Department for Work and Pensions

Research Report No 409

Working with JOT 18 months on: Qualitative research in former Option 1 Pilot Districts

Steve Johnson and Alex Nunn

A report of research carried out by the Policy Research Institute at Leeds Metropolitan University on behalf of the Department for Work and Pensions

Corporate Document Services

Application for reproduction should be made in writing to The Copyright Unit, Her Majesty's Stationery Office, St Clements House, 2-16 Colegate, Norwich NR3 1BQ.

First Published 2007.

ISBN   978 1 84712 149 3

Printed by Corporate Document Services.

Contents

List of tables

List of figures

Acknowledgements

The research underpinning this report was undertaken by a team of researchers from the Policy Research Institute at Leeds Metropolitan University, comprising:

- Dr Steve Johnson (Project Director);

- Dr Alex Nunn (Project Manager);

- Dr Tim Bickerstaffe;

- Mark Rudd;

- Sarah Kelsey;

- Sally-Anne Halliday;

- Penny Wymer (Fieldwork manager);

- James Clarke;

- John Jinks;

- Judith Harvey; and

- Sue Green.

The research team would like to acknowledge the input and support of thank Clare Morley and Phil Smith from the Research Strategy Team in the Performance Measurement and Analysis Division of the Department for Work and Pensions. The JOT Steering Group also provided useful comments and assistance.

Thanks are also due to the large number of fieldwork respondents who participated in the research. These included more than 230 customers, 40 Jobcentre Plus Staff, 24 employers and respondents from 20 providers. We would like to express our appreciation and gratitude for the help and assistance that all the respondents provided in both organising the fieldwork and providing the valuable information, insight and opinion on which this report is based.

The Authors

Dr Alex Nunn is Principal Research Fellow at the Policy Research Institute at Leeds Metropolitan University. His work focuses on social inclusion, welfare to work and governance. He has undertaken a wide range of applied research projects for a range of government departments and public bodies.

Dr Steve Johnson is Director of the Policy Research Institute and Associate Dean of the Faculty of Business and Law at Leeds Metropolitan University. He has undertaken a range of studies for Jobcentre Plus and has published widely on topics such as enterprise, skills, labour market policy and economic development.

Dr Tim Bickerstaffe is Research Fellow at the Policy Research Institute at Leeds Metropolitan University. Formerly the Director of Research at the Low Pay Unit, his work and expertise focus on labour market policy and in particular on low pay and social inclusion.

Summary

Background and introduction

In April 2006 Jobcentre Plus rolled out the Job Outcome Target (JOT) performance measurement system across all Jobcentre Plus districts. The decision to roll out JOT was taken after an extensive piloting exercise in which two distinct variations of the JOT model were applied in seven Pilot districts. The Policy Research Institute, Leeds Metropolitan University, undertook a detailed qualitative evaluation of the introduction of JOT in the Option 1 and Option 2 districts and, together with evidence from the in-house quantitative evaluation, this suggested that JOT was a workable alternative to the then existing performance measurement system.

The final decision was to roll out Option 1 of JOT nationwide. The Option 1 districts have now had more than 18 months' experience of operating under JOT, which should by the time of this research have much more firmly 'bedded-in'. This 'follow-on' evaluation was intended to document and review the impact of JOT in a 'steady state' situation and to assess the contribution that has been made to pursuing the wider objectives of Jobcentre Plus.

Methodology

The aim of the research was to determine if JOT is working as intended in the Option 1 Pilot districts.

The research sought to address this overall aim in the context of the extent to which JOT is supporting the wider aims and objectives of Jobcentre Plus, in particular the Welfare to Work and Channels Strategies and the approach to engagement with employers and providers of training and support to jobseekers and inactive benefit claimants.

The research pursued these objectives via the following methods:

- interviews with more than 40 Jobcentre Plus staff across four Pilot districts;
- interviews with Regional Performance Managers with responsibility for those districts;
- interviews and focus groups with more than 100 customers from all Priority Groups;
- interviews with 24 targeted employers in each of the Option 1 Pilot districts;
- interviews with 20 providers in each of the districts, covering both contracted and non-contracted providers.

Each of these fieldwork tasks was undertaken using a bespoke structured discussion guide.

Findings

The findings from the research are grouped into three broad areas according to the extent to which JOT supports:

- the Welfare to Work Strategy;
- the Channels Strategy;
- the approach to engaging with employers and providers.

Support for the Welfare to Work Strategy

The Welfare to Work Strategy, which aims to make work pay, tackle long-term inactivity and promote employment as the most effective and sustainable route out of poverty, social exclusion and welfare dependency, has several important implications for the operation of Jobcentre Plus. It involves a shift in the way that the organisation deploys its frontline resources toward self-help for those that are 'job-ready' and are able to find work without intervention, and more intensive assistance to those customers defined as 'hardest to help'. JOT was intended to support this overall approach by removing perverse incentives which had operated under the previous 'Job Entry Target' (JET) system and by providing incentives and motivation for frontline staff to concentrate more intensively on helping the 'hardest to help' customers move closer to the labour market and find work.

The research found that a number of important contextual changes were impacting, or had impacted, on the introduction of JOT and the extent to which JOT could drive the changes to behaviours and working practices that will support the Welfare to Work Strategy. Particularly important were instability and uncertainties in the organisation and level of staffing.

However, the findings from the research suggest that **JOT is broadly supportive of the Welfare to Work Strategy**. JOT itself was widely associated with an increasing focus of staff time and energy on the hardest-to-help customers. Specifically, it was reported that JOT led to a decreasing focus on submitting **all** customers for **any** job in the hope that high volumes of submissions would lead to a steady flow of job entries. Instead, Advisers reported that JOT helped to enable them to spend more time with customers, to refer them to more appropriate provision and to overcome their barriers to work, ultimately helping them to move into more sustainable employment. While it was reported that Advisers felt under less pressure to submit customers to jobs immediately, there was no indication that they saw this as a detraction from the overall Welfare to Work message of 'work first'.

It was widely reported that JOT had removed perverse incentives which had operated under the JET system, making the distribution of discretionary financial support to those customers moving from benefits into work more appropriate and less widely used. In addition, JET had often led to intensive competition, sometimes acrimony, between individual staff in Jobcentre Plus offices, undermining team work and the quality of service to customers. JOT was thought to have removed these pressures, leading to enhanced team working, sharing of good practice and better advice and support to customers. Jobcentre Plus staff also noted that they spent much less time than previously, under JET, on following-up employers to track performance data, a finding which was corroborated by evidence from employers. While this was reported to be in line with the need to realise efficiency savings within Jobcentre Plus, it was also felt by some that less frequent contact with employers was a barrier to the collection of evidence which might identify where customers are not actively seeking work, which to an extent undermines the Welfare to Work approach.

Because JET had been so deeply embedded in the Jobcentre Plus organisational culture, it was feared that the introduction of JOT, which removed daily individual level outcome performance data, might undermine the capacity for individual and performance management. There was some evidence to suggest that the new, more qualitative, approaches to individual and performance management that are appropriate under JOT are taking time to bed in, particularly in the light of changes to staffing structures and levels. However, the transition to the use of a broader range of performance management information, including qualitative tools, has also been hampered by the reliance of many managers on one aspect of a recently (at JOT roll-out) introduced performance management tool: the Adviser Achievement Tool (AAT). The AAT was accompanied by the introduction of Key Management Indicators (KMIs) and itself contains a number of indicators of Adviser performance. However, staff and managers reported a widespread reliance on the submissions indicator – and target – which is incorporated within the AAT. This was reported to be undermining the role of JOT in driving the increased focus on the hardest-to-help and the move away from volume submissions to more targeted help and support to customers to help them make the transition to work. In order to meet the submissions target, some staff reported that they saw an incentive to work with job-ready customers or to submit harder to help customers to less appropriate vacancies rather than referring them to the type of support that they need. While this behaviour was only just starting to emerge at the time of the fieldwork, there were widespread concerns and confusion about the implications of this.

Support for the Jobcentre Plus Channels Strategy

The Jobcentre Plus Channels Strategy aims to improve the efficiency of service delivery by steering job-ready customers to self-service channels while focusing staff time on the hardest-to-help customers. JOT was thought to be in line with this strategy by removing the incentive, that JET had provided, to work with job-ready customers in order to claim individual performance points.

A number of changes had been made in the Jobcentre Plus districts to support this strategy such as changes to the structure of staffing, initiatives to reduce the amount of 'footfall' within Jobcentre Plus offices and measures to more effectively identify those that require 'face-to-face' support. This wide number of alternative causal influences meant that it was difficult to attribute changing staff behaviour in relation to self-service channels to JOT. However, while **JOT was widely reported to be consistent with the objectives of the Channels Strategy**, it was not thought to be the most important causal dynamic.

Previous JOT evaluations have suggested that Jobcentre Plus staff have in the past been uncomfortable with referring some customers to self-service channels and were often reluctant to do so. While, this was still evident among some staff, there was a noticeable trend toward increased acceptance of the role to be played by self-service channels. While this was, to an extent, linked to an apparent increasing confidence in the quality of service provided by these channels, there is also scope to conclude that the supportive role that JOT plays may increase over time as the behaviour, working practices and culture associated with JOT become embedded. Customers also had some concerns over the quality of service provided by some of the self-help channels but also appeared to be generally comfortable with the change in service provision and few had noticed any changes in the quality of service that could be attributed to JOT.

Support for employer engagement and relationships with providers

Work with both employers and Jobcentre Plus staff suggested that JOT is in line with decreasing the amount of Jobcentre Plus resource dedicated to contacting employers simply to track performance data. Jobcentre Plus staff generally welcomed this as allowing them to use their time more effectively and **some employers commented positively that they welcomed the reduction in the administrative burden** that this had placed on them. However, Jobcentre Plus staff and employers worried equally that the less frequent contact between local Advisers and employers marked a potential decline in the quality of service offered both to employers and to jobseekers. Despite this, the small number of interviews conducted with employers offered very little evidence of any other changes in Jobcentre Plus activity that could be associated with JOT and most were unaware of any change in the performance measurement system.

Work with both providers and Jobcentre Plus staff suggested that the impact of JOT on the relationship between them was overshadowed by more significant changes in the contracting approach during the Pilot period. This meant that there was very little evidence gathered of any changes to the relationship that could be attributed to JOT. The main exception to this was the **increased willingness of Advisers to refer to non-contracted provision** and an increased level of demand for knowledge about the availability of non-contracted provision that might help customers make the transition to work. Nevertheless, this was again only partly driven by JOT and a more significant cause is likely to have been changes to the level of contracted provision available to Advisers.

Implications of key findings

These key findings suggest a number of implications for the development of policy and management procedures:

- The need for **organisational and institutional stability** in relation to staffing and organisational structures and in messages about appropriate staff behaviour. It is important to bear in mind that Jobcentre Plus has a deeply embedded organisational and cultural commitment to the use of performance indicators and within the organisation there is a tendency to utilise headline measures, despite some concerns about their quality. As such, additional care needs to be given to ensuring that performance management tools, like the AAT, are used appropriately and are accompanied by guidance which makes clear that a balanced approach to measuring individual and team performance is most effective and that under JOT qualitative performance management is at least as important as the use of quantitative headline data.

- To continue to **clarify and reinforce messages with staff** about the linkages between JOT and the wider organisational objectives of Jobcentre Plus in relation to the government's Welfare to Work Strategy and the initiatives within Jobcentre Plus that support this, such as the Channels Strategy and approaches to employer engagement. These messages need to clearly establish the assumptions about what inputs lead to desirable outcomes and managers throughout the hierarchy of the organisation are to ensure that frontline delivery reflects these.

- **Review AAT and its relationship with JOT**, in particular, ensuring that managers at all levels understand and accept the need for a broader and balanced approach to the use of both quantitative and qualitative information.

- Continued **improvement of self-help channels** to ensure that these are able to cope with increased demand and satisfy the needs of customers, avoiding 'bounce-back' to face-to-face channels and disillusionment with job search.

- Continued emphasis on **building and sustaining staff and organisational capacity** in support of the emphasis of JOT on desirable behaviour. At Adviser level this relates to the types of advice, submissions and referrals behaviour desired and the skills and knowledge required to implement this. At Adviser Manager level this relates to the capacity of Adviser Managers to undertake qualitative assessment, interpret a range of quantitative input data and support, coach and mentor individual and groups of Advisers. At district and regional level, this involves an understanding of the messages and meaning of performance data and the need to consider this in relation to other, more qualitative, information and to give appropriate guidance and support to staff lower down in the hierarchy in using this.

- Attention will need to be given to the **skills of the new Adviser Managers** and to ensuring that they have the skills and experience necessary to operate effectively in a JOT environment.

- Continual review of the impact of JOT on **employer contact, customer service and relations with providers**. In particular, staff need to be supported in maintaining appropriate levels of contact with employers to ensure that the two-way flow of information is sufficient for employers' needs to be met and Jobcentre Plus staff to understand the local labour market and be able to target small scale follow-up activities to support customers and to identify customers who may not be fulfilling their obligations to seek work. Staff also need to be increasingly aware of the range of provision (contracted and non-contracted) available within their localities to meet the varying needs of customers.

1 Introduction

1.1 Introduction and background

In April 2006 Jobcentre Plus rolled out the Job Outcome Target (JOT) performance management system across all Jobcentre Plus districts. The decision to roll-out JOT was taken after an extensive piloting exercise in which two distinct variations of the JOT model were applied in seven Pilot districts. A team of researchers at the Policy Research Institute, Leeds Metropolitan University, undertook a detailed four-phase qualitative evaluation of the introduction of JOT in the Option 1 and Option 2 districts and found that:

> *'JOT is feasible as an alternative approach to performance measurement and management for Jobcentre Plus'*

and recommended that:

> *'JOT should be rolled out on a national basis as soon as is operationally possible.'*

> (Johnson and Nunn, 2005).

Following the advice of both the qualitative and quantitative evaluations (the latter was conducted in-house by Jobcentre Plus Analytical Division) the decision was made to roll-out a version of JOT which closely resembled that piloted in the Option 1 districts. These Option 1 districts have now had more than 18 months' experience of operating under JOT, which should by now have much more firmly 'bedded-in'. This 'follow-on' evaluation was intended to document and review the impact of JOT in a 'steady state' and to assess the contribution that has been made to pursuing the wider objectives of Jobcentre Plus. The report, thus, addresses the contribution of JOT in relation to the Government's wider Welfare to Work Strategy, the Jobcentre Plus Channels Strategy and the engagement of Jobcentre Plus with both employers and providers of training and employment support.

1.2   The rationale for JOT

JOT differs substantially from the previous Job Entry Target (JET) performance management regime in a number of significant respects:

- JET only aimed to attribute performance 'points' to Jobcentre Plus where an individual entered work as a direct result of a Jobcentre Plus intervention. As such, Jobcentre Plus had to 'prove' that an intervention had taken place to ensure that performance would be attributed;

- JET attributed job entry points to individual members of staff;

- job entry points could be calculated on an almost immediate basis, with staff and offices often monitoring performance on a daily basis.

These characteristics of JET were felt to have a number of important drawbacks resulting in some possible 'perverse incentives'. In some cases, individual staff would seek to generate an intervention where one was not needed to help a client move into work, so that job entry points could be claimed. This led to instances where a client who had found their own job would be offered some unnecessary assistance (such as training provision or financial payments) so that Jobcentre Plus could claim that as their own job entry. In addition, JET did not always capture the full extent of Jobcentre Plus performance in cases where employment was found through self-service channels or where administrative error made it difficult to prove that an intervention had taken place. Taken together this meant that a great deal of Jobcentre Plus resource was put into ensuring that rigid and often superfluous administrative practices were followed for the sole purpose of performance reporting rather than actually helping clients find work.

By contrast, JOT counts evidence of all 'job outcomes', measured as 'off-flows' from benefits and into employment. This is achieved through the use of HM Revenue and Customs data on income tax accounts. This means that Jobcentre Plus is able to make efficiency savings while simultaneously being able to maintain frontline services and delivery. JOT is also intended to ensure that the full range of performance is allocated to Jobcentre Plus, acknowledging the much wider use of 'self-service' channels such as electronic job points and warm phones to Jobcentre Plus call centres. Because of this, JOT is not able to attribute job outcomes to individual staff or even to identifiable Jobcentre Plus offices. The combined result is that JOT was intended to support the prioritisation of the organisation's resources on those deemed to be in the most need of help and to refer those most likely to be able to help themselves to the self-help channels, through the removal of the incentive to work with those that are easiest to place in work. To support this, JOT, like JET, allocates differential levels of points to Jobcentre Plus based on a customer's 'priority group'.

Therefore, the introduction of JOT was intended to be part of the broader effort to modernise Jobcentre Plus, creating a more efficient organisation where resources are prioritised to help those customers in the greatest need, in line with the Department for Work and Pension's Public Service Agreement target.

1.3   Summary of findings from the Pilots evaluation

The JOT Pilot districts were subject to both an external qualitative and an internal quantitative evaluation. The synthesis report which reported on the combined findings (Johnson and Nunn, 2005a), found the following:

- JOT contributed to increased efficiency, primarily through reduced follow-up activity and reduced use of the Adviser Discretionary Fund (ADF);

- JOT complemented the shift to self-help channels for some customer groups;

- JOT had the potential to enable the organisation to focus more of its resources on the most disadvantaged client groups;

- JOT required a major cultural shift and drove radically different staff behaviour, including a more qualitative approach to performance and management;

- Jobcentre Plus needed to invest in the capacity of the organisation to deliver the changed working and management practices required under JOT;

- the impact of JOT on employers and providers was minimal at the Pilot stage;

- though it was difficult to be conclusive, the impact of JOT had no more than a small negative impact on the quality of service to some customer groups.

1.4   Organisational change

The Pilot evaluation studies emphasised that JOT required a major change in the underlying culture of Jobcentre Plus. It disrupted widely and deeply held assumptions about the type, nature and quantity of input interventions that drive recorded outcome performance and led to widespread questioning of how these might be revised. It was, thus, clear that JOT could not become fully embedded during the Pilot phase and in many cases the speed of transition to the new system proved surprising in the Pilots evaluation. After 18 months of experience in operating under JOT, it was hoped that the follow-on evaluation could assess, in a more rounded way, the extent to which JOT has become embedded. However, while this attempt was for the most part successful, it is worth noting at the outset that even now, there is some cause for caution over expectations of the change that was possible, as a result of the sheer scale of organisational change required by accommodating JOT.

2 Evaluation methodology

2.1 Aims of the evaluation

The aim of this research was to determine if Job Outcome Target (JOT) is working as intended in the Option 1 Pilot districts, 18 months after implementation.

With the principal objectives of:

- establishing what working behaviours/patterns have emerged as a result of working with JOT for 18 months;

- highlighting specific working processes specifically developed and implemented to help ensure the achievement of JOT;

- determining the intended and unintended outcomes of JOT in relation to staff, customers and employers;

- assessing how, if at all, the national roll out of JOT has impacted on JOT operations within the Pilot areas.

The research sought to answer these questions within the parameters of the extent to which JOT is operating in line with the wider aims and objectives of Jobcentre Plus in supporting the:

- Jobcentre Plus Channels Strategy;

- Jobcentre Plus Employer Engagement Strategy; and

- wider Welfare to Work Strategy.

2.2 Methods

The research included a variety of components. Each of these are described under the relevant headings below.

2.2.1 Interviews with Jobcentre Plus staff

Interviews were held with more than 40 Jobcentre Plus staff, including:

- ten members of staff in each Option 1 Pilot district (Devon, Calderdale & Kirklees, North West Wales and Lambeth, Southwark & Wandsworth) to cover a range of responsibilities including District Manager (or Deputy), Performance Manager, at least one Business Manager, Adviser Manager(s), Team Leader(s), Advisers, frontline staff and individuals who have dealings with employers;

- Regional Performance Managers for each of the four regions containing Option 1 Pilot districts

Interviews were conducted on a face-to-face basis where possible, though a small number were conducted by telephone where this was more appropriate to the availability of the respondent.

Interviews lasted between 45 and 60 minutes, and followed a structured discussion guide which was agreed in advance with Jobcentre Plus Analytical Division prior to the fieldwork. The discussion guide is shown in Appendix A. Interviews were recorded (with the agreement of respondents) to provide back-up for interviewer notes and enable the use of direct (unattributed) quotes in this report.

2.2.2 Interviews and focus groups with customers

It was important to explore the views and experiences of a range of customers who might have been affected in different ways by JOT. In general, the intention and expectation underpinning JOT is that it should result in more intensive work with customers in higher priority groups and that lower priority group customers should be encouraged to utilise the available self-help channels for their job search activities. JOT is also expected and intended to affect processes such as the volume and nature of submissions for vacancies and the use of external providers, partners and agencies to enhance the employability of higher priority group customers.

The research included two related data collection exercises with customers in the four Option 1 districts, one with Priority Group (PG) 1, 2 and 3 customers and the other with PG4 and PG5 customers:

- **Focus groups with PG1, 2 and 3 customers** – three focus groups were held with PG1, 2 and 3 customers respectively in each Option 1 district to explore the extent to which clients in these priority groups perceive any changes in the quality of services offered to them. Each focus group lasted between 60 and 90 minutes. In total, 110 customers participated in the research (see Table 2.1). Participants were offered a small cash gift and travel expenses and childcare to ensure that a wide range of views could be canvassed. Jobcentre Plus provided a random sample of 100 customers for each of the priority groups. The initial sample was selected for geographical proximity to Jobcentre Plus offices and the Focus Group location to secure high take-up. The full sample was invited to take part in the Focus Group by postal invitation. Neutral venues with full disabled access were identified in which to hold each session. For each session a maximum of 12 places were available, with those customers who returned invitation letters autonomously being contacted first to discuss their availability to attend the session. Once these customers had been contacted, remaining places were filled by follow-up telephone invitations. Customers who had not returned their proformas were telephoned and invited to attend. As we needed to ensure that each group contained a mix of customers by age, gender and, for the PG1 only, benefit type, the customers contacted by telephone were specifically selected to balance the characteristics of those already booked for the group.

- **Interviews with PG4 and PG5 customers** – identification of these customers was not straightforward and was undertaken in the form of a 'traffic survey' in Jobcentre Plus offices. The survey eventually covered 124 clients from these customer groups across the four Option 1 Pilot districts, though it was not sampled for quantitative analysis and all findings have been interpreted and analysed using qualitative methods only. Discussions were held with the JOT lead officer in each district to determine the two most appropriate office locations and permission was sought in advance from the office manager. Two interviewers attended each site from opening until closing time on the agreed date. Interviewers approached potential interviewees as they left the office to first of all establish if they were a PG4 or PG5 customer and, if so, they were invited to participate in the interview

In all cases, customer interviews and focus groups were undertaken via a specifically designed structured discussion guide and questionnaire (see Appendices B and C, respectively). Filter questions were used to ensure that clients were able to compare the service they received during the Pilot period and after national roll-out.

Table 2.1 Numbers of customers from priority groups who participated in the research

District	Customer group					Total
	PG1	PG2	PG3	PG4	PG5	
Calderdale & Kirklees	5	7	9	15	21	57
Devon	7	11	9	14	21	62
Lambeth, Southwark & Wandsworth	11	11	11	17	18	68
North West Wales & Powys	9	12	8	6	12	47
Total	32	41	37	52	72	234

2.2.3 Interviews with employers

A small number (24) of targeted interviews were undertaken with a cross-section of employers in each of the Option 1 districts who have links with Jobcentre Plus. The majority of these interviews were undertaken by telephone and again used a structured discussion guide, which is shown in Appendix D. The selection of employers for the interviews was undertaken randomly from district-level databases.

2.2.4 Interviews with providers

Twenty interviews were conducted with a cross-section of providers in each of the Option 1 districts who have links with Jobcentre Plus in either a contracted or non-contracted capacity. All of these interviews were conducted by telephone and the structured discussion guide is shown in Appendix D.

3   Support for the Welfare to Work Strategy

3.1   Key elements of the Welfare to Work Strategy

Since 1997 the government has pursued a 'Welfare to Work' strategy. The key themes of this have been:

- **Making work pay** – Several initiatives, such as the introduction of the National Minimum Wage and Tax Credits have aimed to ensure that there are clear financial incentives to reward the transition from unemployment, inactivity and benefits dependency to work. These policies have aimed to address the widely recognised operation of poverty traps (Treasury, 1998:29-36).

- **Employment first policies** – The Welfare to Work agenda has gradually increased the emphasis on work as the most effective and sustainable route out of poverty and welfare dependency. The approach has been pursued through the Jobseeker's Allowance (JSA) regime and New Deal programmes of assistance and support to help people to move into work. National programmes like New Deal have gradually been augmented by various geographically targeted programmes of support to help people make the transition to work such as Working Neighbourhoods Pilots, Employment Zones and Action Teams for Jobs. The approach taken has included both support in the form of employment and job-search advice, work-focused training and assistance with some of the costs associated with starting work (such as small amounts of financial assistance to buy clothes or to pay for travel to work in the initial period of employment). For those who are capable of work participation in these programmes of assistance has been compulsory and refusal to participate (through attending meetings with Personal Advisers or New Deal Training programmes) has incurred the potential for financial sanction. So, while New Deal programmes have been targeted at a variety of specific groups such as young people, older people and disabled people, the compulsory element has been restricted to JSA claimants.

- **Tackling inactivity** – More recently, the employment-first approach has been expanded from unemployed to inactive benefit claimants. Previously, the employment-first approach had been largely limited to JSA claimants. Since 2005, however, there has been an increasing emphasis on expanding the work-first approach to inactive benefit claimants through the expansion of the Pathways to Work model and the replacement of Incapacity Benefit with a new Employment Support Allowance and Personal Capacity Assessment which are proposed in the Welfare Reform Bill. The introduction of age discrimination legislation and changes to pensions legislation is also intended to allow older workers to remain in the labour market for longer.

The pursuit of the Welfare to Work Strategy has been accompanied by rising rates of employment in the UK and the government has recently committed itself to an ambitious target of reaching an 80 per cent employment rate.

This strategy has had important implications for Jobcentre Plus. Jobcentre Plus contributes to the Welfare to Work Strategy by promoting work as the best form of welfare, helping unemployed and inactive people to compete for work. Jobcentre Plus is also required to help those with barriers to employment identify ways of overcoming these and moving closer to the labour market. A primary implication of this is the imperative to work more intensively and effectively with the 'hardest to help' customer groups. It also means ensuring that those customer groups that are able to help themselves into work are increasingly referred to self-help channels (this is discussed in Chapter 4).

The introduction of the Job Outcome Target (JOT) to replace the Job Entry Target (JET) was intended to remove perverse incentives under the old performance management system which might have prevented Jobcentre Plus staff from changing their behaviour to fit the Welfare to Work Strategy. The rationale for the introduction of JOT was that it would allow staff to pursue the most appropriate intervention for the individual service user, including referral to other staff or external agencies. The following discussion focuses on the extent to which JOT has helped to support the overall Welfare to Work Strategy in the Pilot districts. It relies, in the main, on evidence from discussions with Jobcentre Plus staff, though where relevant, evidence from interviews and focus groups with service users is also drawn upon.

3.2   Contextual changes

In assessing the role of JOT in supporting the Welfare to Work agenda it is necessary to also understand other contextual changes in the Pilot districts which might have had an impact on the role, influence and contribution of JOT. The qualitative case study fieldwork explored national, regional and local issues that might have impacted in this way.

A number of national issues were identified. The continuing impact of current reforms and reorganisation of Jobcentre Plus related to the need to achieve efficiency savings and cost reductions were thought to have impacted negatively on the capacity of the districts to implement JOT reforms. For instance, in one district, the Pilot phase of JOT had coincided with the need to reduce headcount by around 200. This had only been partially achieved at the time of the follow-on evaluation fieldwork. The district was still waiting for ministerial decisions regarding the closure of Jobcentre Plus offices meaning that the district staffing resources are overstretched despite some districts reporting the need to reduce their staffing level further. This has an obvious impact on the capacity of districts to manage organisational change and to implement the performance management initiatives required under JOT, such as increased qualitative monitoring of Adviser activity. As the initial Pilot evaluation of JOT also highlighted (Johnson and Nunn, 2005), the impact of such changes on staff morale and motivation had a bearing on the operational capacity of Jobcentre Plus. There was some continuing evidence in the follow-on evaluation fieldwork that this was still an important issue facing the organisation.

The impact of efficiency initiatives on the capacity of the districts was compounded by other workforce changes and instability. For instance, in one district the JOT Pilot had occurred simultaneously to a district-wide workforce planning process which had led to very high (46 per cent) levels of turnover among Advisers. In another district, under-staffing had resulted in around 100 staff being recruited through transfers from other districts and temporary recruitment. In addition, since national roll-out Jobcentre Plus has restructured its management structure with the introduction of several new functional roles.

The impact of this is that Advisory Management Services have been given separate line management responsibilities, potentially covering several sites. To recognise the increased responsibility at this level, these posts have been reallocated to a more senior grade in the organisational hierarchy. The implication, however, is that many of the staff that had been responsible for managing Advisers during the Pilots are no longer in this role and more senior staff are now undertaking these tasks.

These two changes are important because Pilot districts had undertaken considerable training and development of both Advisers and Adviser Managers to revise their roles as part of the introduction of JOT. The loss of experienced Advisers means that much of this training has to be repeated and some important skills and experience has been lost. The change in the nature of Adviser Managers has similar implications. However, it is also important because the overall impact of this change is that those responsible for managing the performance of Advisers have less recent experience of undertaking the Adviser role itself. Taken together, these changes in the staffing structure may have had a key bearing on the stability of the Pilot districts and their capacity to manage performance; because both Advisers and Adviser Managers are the key staff groups to achieve delivery under JOT. Certainly respondents in at least one district noted that this was a constraint on their organisational capacity.

Other major national influences that may have affected operational delivery included the combination of the transition to an intensified work-first approach through the refresh of JSA and rising JSA and unemployment register. For instance, one Jobcentre Plus Business Manager commented on her perception that she was being asked to devote more time to addressing new JSA claimants confused the overall message about appropriate behaviour that JOT was intended to support. She identified the renewed emphasis on JSA claimants as confusing, detracting from the message that Jobcentre Plus is to increasingly focus its operational effort on the hardest-to-help service users. Confusion over priorities was also felt to arise from the introduction of a submissions target in the Adviser Achievement Tool (AAT) and the emphasis that was placed on Advisers and Adviser Managers to ensure an average rate of submissions per interview. This was a major issue and attracted strong and robust comment from many respondents.

In terms of JOT delivery, some national labour market trends were thought to be particularly important in some districts. For instance, one district reported major implications arising from new economic migrants to the UK, especially from those countries that have recently acceded to the European Union. This has had a major impact on the capacity of some districts to place priority customer groups in entry-level work because of the increased competition for these jobs from these new migrant workers. This was thought to be doubly important in the context of a perception among some respondents of a falling level of Jobcentre Plus vacancies. Department for Work and Pensions statistics suggest that the national picture in relation to vacancies is complicated, however. Generally rising levels of notified vacancies (inflows) since the spring of 2006 have combined with a falling 'stock' of live vacancies over the summer months as a result of strong flows of vacancies off Jobcentre Plus records.

As in the previous evaluation of JOT, several influences were also thought to reinforce the overall contribution of JOT to the Welfare to Work Strategy. These included the 'footfall' project, the introduction and strengthening of self-help channels (e.g. Job Points and 'Warm Phones' and the increasing use of Job Seeker Direct) for those service users deemed to be capable of helping themselves. While these broader changes in the operation and priorities of Jobcentre Plus were widely thought to be closely aligned with the introduction of JOT, they did, in many cases, lead to difficulties in attribution and causality as to whether it was JOT or these other changes that had driven changes in support of the Welfare to Work approach.

At the local level, there are several factors which impact on the scope for JOT to drive changes in operational practices which are supportive of the Welfare to Work Strategy. These include for instance, general reductions in the amount of contracted provision. The amount, type and quality of training and other provision available is an aggravated problem in rural and remote districts. The result of such shortages is that the scope for JOT to encourage increased referral to providers is severely constrained.

3.3   Staff awareness and understanding

The extent to which Jobcentre Plus respondents understood the relationship between JOT and the Welfare to Work Strategy was complex. On one hand, many staff were clearly confused about their contribution to the district-level outcome target, especially in relation to their quantitative contribution of number of job outcomes achieved. The initial evaluation of JOT suggested that the lack of individual and office level performance data and delays in the availability of timely district-level data was a cause of some uncertainty among staff. Evidence from the follow-on fieldwork suggested that this continues to be the case. In addition, few staff were aware or understood how district-level targets were calculated or arrived at and some were concerned that the targets had been increased substantially over the last year. Understanding and awareness of how targets were calculated varied between districts at district management level.

Importantly, however, the way in which they failed to understand their contribution to the district target appeared to be more related to outcome-performance than it was to a lack of understanding about appropriate behaviour. Indeed, most staff reported that they understood the revised emphasis on inputs and behaviour rather than on outcomes under JOT. The Pilot districts had put considerable work and resources into clarifying the expectations of Advisers and Adviser Managers through the establishment and development of Adviser strategies. As a result of this effort, staff tended to be clear that under JOT, the expectation is that they will focus their attention on the hardest-to-help customers and that they are no longer under pressure to submit these groups to vacancies regardless of their prospects of success. Staff were aware that JOT was intended to ensure that this group of service users were to be helped to move closer to the labour market. However, they were also aware that the ultimate objective was to encourage service users to overcome their barriers and make the transition to work.

Recent changes in the intensity of the work-first message in the Welfare to Work approach had, though, caused some confusion about how these objectives were to be pursued. Some staff, therefore, reported confusion over the renewed priority being given to dealing with JSA claimants and to making submissions, as measured and driven through the AAT.

3.4   Motivation, behaviour and working practices

3.4.1   Staff motivation

The previous target system (JET) had included powerful and regular incentives in the form of the Daily Placing List of job entries and job entries were a deeply embedded part of the culture of Jobcentre Plus. The initial evaluation, including the results of fieldwork prior to JOT 'going live', demonstrated that staff and managers were anxious about the impact that the loss of timely and individualised outcome performance data would have on individual motivations. In particular, there were concerns that some Advisers would be able to 'hide' as a result of the removal of the scrutiny that individual level outcome performance data brings. The evidence provided in the initial evaluation was inconclusive on this issue, with little firm or substantive evidence of motivation declining as a result of JOT.

During the follow-on fieldwork, both staff and managers reported that Advisers and other frontline staff have to be more self-managing and self-motivating as a result of the replacement of JET with JOT. Again, though, the evidence on this issue suggested that the impact of the loss of daily performance data was complex and affected different individuals in varying ways. While some Advisers were now less motivated, a larger number felt liberated by the removal of the focus on job entries and were able to more effectively channel their activity to overcoming the barriers faced by the hardest-to-help:

> *'I say "look I would rather you picked up on the barrie, and addressed it than tick all the boxes on the interview", and if you have to see that person again, that's fine, we seem to have built more flexibility into diaries and I think Advisers are more empowered to make their own decisions over what the best way forward is.'*

(Jobcentre Plus Business Manager)

Among this group, helping service users was thought to be a more powerful motivation. JOT was thought to have removed previous perverse incentives, with the result that staff were now more motivated to address barriers to work, for instance through more appropriate referrals to a wider range of training and other provision.

However, others continued to report some sense of loss of motivation as a result of the loss of immediate outcome performance data and the 'buzz' that this provided:

> *'We have become less performance focused in a way, I kind of liked it before when we could put the job entry placings up, we could say "yes we have achieved", there was definitely more excitement before… and more drive whereas now because we don't really know how we are doing…we have lost that drive a bit, I feel.'*

(Jobcentre Plus Adviser Manager)

For those that might have been demotivated as a result of the introduction of JOT, though, the introduction of the AAT (see Section 3.6) and the range of additional performance measures such as Key Management Indicators (KMIs) and Quality Assurance Frameworks has had a motivating impact. Indeed, one Team Leader reported that:

> *'None of them want to end up on an Improvement Plan.'*

(Jobcentre Plus Team Leader)

However, there was some concern about the capacity of the organisation to make the best use of these tools, principally due to a lack of staff and skills (see Section 3.7).

3.4.2   Working with the hardest-to-help

The impact of JOT was thought to free up time to work more intensively and effectively with the hardest-to-help service users. There was thought to be less emphasis on immediate submissions and more emphasis on gradually moving those service users that had the most fundamental barriers closer to the labour market (see 3.4.3). Advisers also felt that the impact of JOT has been to allow them to be more flexible, especially in sourcing the most effective provision and help for clients to overcome their barriers to employment (see Section 4).

3.4.3   Submissions activity

Staff and managers across the districts were unanimous in their view that the introduction of JOT had been accompanied by an apparent and immediate reduction in the level of submissions activity; a finding which is confirmed by consideration of the available quantitative data on submissions activity. The reasons for this were related to both an actual reduction in the level of submissions made and also reduced attention to recording.

Staff reported that in spending increased time with the hardest-to-help customers and being relieved of the responsibility of chasing job entries the rate of submissions would naturally fall. However, they argued forcefully that this was about increasing the quality of submissions through both improving the extent to which service users had been helped to move genuinely closer to the labour market and improving the effort and attention paid to the quality of job matching.

> *'There is not that quick fix mentality anymore, that you would be looking more at sustainability and looking more at is this person really what that employer wants and needs, can they cope with this sort of work, if they are very close to it, then that is where the intervention with the employer* [is relevant]*, using things like work trials…'*

(Jobcentre Plus Business Manager)

Though the evaluation involved no methodological tool to judge the validity of such claims, it is certainly consistent to argue that increasing the amount of genuine assistance to move the hardest-to-help service users toward sustainable entry to work would reduce the volume of submissions activity. This would also ultimately be a more efficient method of delivering employment advice and support. This is because previous assumptions about the rate of job entries that could be achieved by a given level of submissions, led to wasted effort submitting job seekers to vacancies that they could not hope to gain, wasting the time, energy (and potentially motivation) of staff, job seekers themselves and employers. These old assumptions might also have led to individual job seekers gaining employment before genuinely overcoming their barriers to work, with the result that they would quickly return to unemployment or inactivity and be recycled through the system. The consequence would obviously be to further boost submissions activity. This means that JOT should have been expected to have reduced the level of submissions activity and as was reported in the initial evaluation; revised assumptions will need to be formed about the level of Jobcentre Plus submissions activity and job outcomes.

In place of these blanket assumptions, some Business Managers reported that there was increased emphasis on researching and understanding the local labour market. Increased labour market intelligence is then used to guide input behaviour and activity:

> 'We would be looking to make sure that people have a knowledge of what is coming in the local labour market, what notified vacancies we had, what is in the papers, a certain amount of trying to keep up with what is going on and what employer does what, who is taking on and who is making redundant.'

(Jobcentre Plus Business Manager)

Jobcentre Plus respondents suggested that the rate of submissions activity had recovered slightly since the initial Pilot period, but was still below the JET level. The recovery of submissions appeared, from the qualitative research, to have occurred in stages. For instance, the initial evaluation also reported an initial dip in submissions activity before a period of recovery. The follow-on fieldwork suggests that there has been a further recovery since that time, especially since national roll-out. Again, this is confirmed by the quantitative data. Evidence from the qualitative fieldwork suggests that this latter recovery is being driven by the introduction of the AAT and specifically the incorporation of a submissions target within it.

The incorporation of this submissions target in particular was widely (though not quite universally) thought to be in significant tension with the role of JOT and its underlying principles. Specifically, it was thought to be in contradiction to the Welfare to Work objective of assisting the hardest-to-help to move closer to the labour market by renewing the pressure on Advisers to make high levels of often inappropriate or poor quality submissions. Further discussion of the AAT is included in Section 3.6.

One potential impact of focusing increased attention on the hardest-to-help service users, is that Jobcentre Plus submissions are more targeted at lower-paid or part-time vacancies. Qualitative discussions with Jobcentre Plus staff produced no evidence to suggest that this is the case.

3.4.4   Use of Adviser Discretionary Fund

One result of JOT is that the discretionary funds (Adviser Discretionary Fund – ADF) available to Advisers to assist job seekers with the transition to work is now more effectively and appropriately used. This is important because the costs associated with the transition to work can be an important barrier to leaving benefits. These transitional costs can be considerable and relate, for instance, to work clothing (including for interviews), special tools or equipment and transport to work costs that often need to be provided prior to receiving wages. The ADF is intended as one means of supporting clients to overcome these barriers through a small one-off payment. However, under JET the distribution of the ADF acted as evidence of a Jobcentre Plus intervention and thus, was often used inappropriately to 'buy' a job entry, with payments being offered to clients who did not require it to enter work (Johnson and Nunn, 2005:26-7).

It was hoped that JOT would remove this perverse incentive and lead to both reduced and more appropriate use of the ADF. As in the initial Pilot evaluation, the evidence from the follow-on fieldwork was that JOT has been successful in this regard. Staff and managers universally reported that the level of ADF expenditure has fallen considerably and it was also widely reported that where it is used, that this is now more appropriate and genuinely related to supporting clients in the transition to work:

> *'As a result of JOT you're not necessarily,… before JOT with JET, people were thinking that I must see if he needs ADF, see if [the customer] wants something, whatever else financially. Whereas with JOT you're not thinking that because that job entry is going to be attributed.'*

(Jobcentre Plus Adviser)

3.4.5   Follow-up with employers

Under JET, considerable energy and resources were used in following up submissions to vacancies as a means of chasing job entry points. One of the key assumed benefits of JOT was to reduce this activity. The initial evaluation found that the introduction of JOT had resulted in reduced follow-up, especially in Option 1 districts, the Pilot version of JOT which was ultimately closest to the model rolled-out. Generally, the follow-on fieldwork suggested that there has been no major change in these findings as JOT has 'bedded-in'. Advisers and managers reported that follow-up activity had reduced. The exception is in the relationship between Employer Engagement Teams and large employers who often still provide follow-up lists in order to help Jobcentre Plus improve the quality of service to these employers.

The general reduction in follow-up activity did, though, have some implications for the overall Welfare to Work Strategy. Advisers reported that follow-up had previously given them a keen insight into the behaviour of job seekers and specifically the extent to which they were actively seeking work. It acted as an information gathering stage in the sanctioning process. Follow-up was also a good way of collecting information about performance at interview and thus, helping service users to improve their employability by providing feedback and coaching. As such, the reduction in follow-up had the impact that Advisers felt generally less aware of whether or not service users were actively seeking work and how they were performing at interview. Both of these consequences of the introduction of JOT might be seen as having negative implications for the pursuit of the wider Welfare to Work Strategy.

Recognising this, however, many Advisers reported that they were flexible in their approach and maintained a low level of follow-up activity where they felt this was appropriate. For instance, where they suspected that a client was not actively seeking work or where a client had been unsuccessful in several interviews they would follow up a submission as a means of collecting further information. This type of follow-up, though, requires a relationship between Advisers and service users and is thus much more likely to be relevant for specific groups of Advisers such as

Incapacity Benefit and Lone Parent Advisers. The overall effect is to partially offset the potential unforeseen and negative implications of reduced overall follow-up in relation to the contribution of JOT toward the Welfare to Work agenda.

An additional reason why Advisers may occasionally follow up submissions, including successful ones, relates to the collection of examples of good performance for performance review purposes. The loss of individual level outcome performance data has shifted the emphasis in individual performance management to more qualitative sources of information and the collection of this by individual staff themselves. Following up successful submissions with both employers and especially service users themselves, thus acts as one means of collecting information for this purpose. This was also encouraged by some Adviser Manager's in an attempt to motivate staff:

> 'If they are long-term unemployed and they just disappear off the register and you don't know where they have gone it is pretty disheartening,… for their own satisfaction and for evidence for their review, in a little way they do [chase destinations] and in a little way I encourage them because I actually think being an Adviser is about job satisfaction and knowing that you have got a positive outcome for someone and if they have just gone of the register, while some people might call that a positive outcome it is nice to know if they have gone into employment and that you have really done something to change their lives and help them.'

(Adviser Manager)

Individual and team performance management is discussed in more detail in Section 3.6.

3.5 Team working and motivation

One of the negative impacts of the JET performance management system had been to discourage team working because of the incentive to retain individual job entry points. Advisers and other frontline staff were, thus, protective of their clients and reluctant to share them with colleagues for fear that they would 'steal' their points. The initial evaluation suggested that there had been improvement in team working, especially among Advisers, as a result of the introduction of JOT. At that point, this had led to increased sharing of labour market information and, in some cases, sharing of good practice.

Evidence from the follow-up evaluation suggests that team working continues to improve. As JOT has become embedded, Advisers have become much more willing to share their clients. As such, clients can often be seen at more convenient times:

> *'Historically if you had customers on your case load you really wanted your name to come up on that placings list. ...so you would try to keep your own customers but now because it all goes into one pot so to speak, I am noticing, whether be it in my team or in my own working practices when your not going to be here or if your diary is fully booked, you are quite willing to give a customer, either to a colleague ...because it is a team target rather than an individual target.'*

(Jobcentre Plus Team Leader)

More importantly, however, in relation to the Welfare to Work approach, the research also found that Advisers were now more likely to pass clients to colleagues where they identified a need that they perceived a colleague may be more able to address, because of their particular social skills, knowledge or expertise:

> *'It has led to better team-working because people are not hanging on to their own customers because "if I don't get the sub in then I don't get the points", so if they feel that another Adviser would be better suited for example to dealing with that customer and some of the ones where perhaps you have been working with them for ages and a certain approach hasn't worked they will hand them of to someone else to see if their approach will work.'*

(Jobcentre Plus Business Manager)

A related finding was that staff were also now less protective of good quality vacancies than under JET. For instance, in the past, where a vacancy that was perceived to be particularly attractive was notified to an office, staff would often attempt to keep it within the office rather than sharing between offices. This is now less likely to be the case.

The follow-on evaluation also found some limited evidence of improved working relationships between different groups of staff. For example, in one district the relationship between job broking and benefit processing staff was thought to have improved. This was thought to arise from the reduced tension and conflict over the allocation of benefit sign-offs to particular Advisers. In another district, the relationship between Employer Engagement Teams and job broking staff was improved. This had developed as Advisers were more willing to use methods that might have been discouraged by JET, such as Work Trials, which requires closer working with Employer Engagement staff.

3.6   Individual and performance management

3.6.1   Performance management under JOT

Several tools are used in performance management under JOT. The first tool is a set of nationally agreed KMIs. These KMIs for the 2006-07 operational year are:

- Adviser Submissions: x per cent of mandatory advisory interviews conducted will result in at least one job submission.

- Contact Centre Activity: Of all telephone calls answered by Jobseeker Direct, 80 per cent will result in at least one job submission

- JSA Interventions: 80 per cent of 13 and 26-week JSA advisory interviews are conducted within six weeks.

- Income Support (IS) Interventions: 80 per cent of initial IS Work Focused Interviews (WFIs), that are booked, are attended. 87 per cent of Lone Parent (LP) WFI reviews, that become due, are booked and conducted within three months.

- IB Interventions: In 90 per cent of cases, the initial Incapacity Benefit (IB) WFI is conducted before the end of ninth week stage of the claim.

These KMIs are supported by an AAT. Generally, the AAT and specifically, the inclusion of a submissions target within it, was almost universally criticised. The AAT is a performance management tool for Business Managers and Adviser Managers to use to assess the performance of Advisers. It includes a wide variety of indicators such as the:

- number of working days in the measurement period;

- amount of that time spent on new jobseeker interviews, restart, JSA New Deal clients, lone parents or IB recipients;

- amount of time spent as a 13-week Adviser;

- amount of experience that an Adviser has;

- number of interviews conducted and the number conducted per day;

- number of job submissions made and the ratio of submissions to interviews;

- number of Better Off (in work) Calculations (BOCs) or In Work Benefit Calculations (IWBCs) undertaken and the ratio of BOCs/IWBCs to interviews.

In addition, the AAT also includes two national targets for Advisers of 60% of all interviews resulting in a submission and 20 per cent of interviews to result in BOCs/IWBCs; and scores Advisers out of ten for their achievement of these targets.

Guidance on the use of the AATs suggests that it is mandatory and that the purpose of the AAT *'is to ensure all our advisers contribute effectively to Jobcentre Plus aims and to identify those advisers who may need more help and support'*. The guidance also suggests that the AAT is based on national standards which are the minimum that an Adviser is expected to achieve. The guidance also states that failure to achieve these should result in the agreement of an Adviser Improvement Plan.

In addition to these quantitative tools, Business and Adviser Managers are supposed to use more qualitative performance management methods under JOT, such as observations of interviews using the Quality Assurance Framework (QAF).

3.6.2 Role of the Adviser Achievement Tool

Fieldwork with respondents in the Pilot districts suggests that the AAT may have become the main way in which the performance of Advisers is measured for many managers, despite the inclusion in the guidance on its use of the qualification that *'adviser managers should not rely on the Adviser Achievement Tool alone to deliver performance improvements'*. It was also clear that both Advisers and many managers dislike the AAT and the inclusion of a specific submissions target in particular. Many respondents reported that the submissions target led to confusion over appropriate behaviour and priorities and detracted from their capacity to focus on the most appropriate interventions to move the hardest-to-help closer to the labour market. They also felt that an implication of this was a renewed incentive to work with PG4 and PG5 who are normally thought to be able to help themselves as a means of raising Adviser's ratio of submissions to interviews. It is difficult to overestimate the strength of feeling on this issue that was encountered in interviews with some Advisers.

Part of the animosity toward the AAT and the submissions target within it may be a result of confusion regarding the ways in which it is to be used. In many cases, Advisers reported that the AAT was used as a one-size fits all tool, when in reality the assumptions about rates of submission needed to be varied by client group. Though this more flexible approach was confirmed as the national expectation in discussions with the JOT steering group, the guidance is ambiguous on the issue and it is easy to understand how this could be misconstrued. districts had also varied the rate of submissions expected from the national standards, raising this from 60 per cent to 70 per cent in one district.

While there is certainly scope for increased clarity about how the AAT is to be used, at least one Regional Performance Manager reported that the inclusion of any type of AAT tool was likely to drive narrowly conceived behaviour:

> *'...an activity had to be chosen... Whatever we'd chosen would have driven the wrong behaviour because if we'd put "referrals to provision", what would we be doing now? – we'd be having endless inappropriate referrals to provision. Whatever activity we'd put in to the AAT would have resulted in the same outcome.'*

(Jobcentre Plus, Regional Performance Manager)

In one district, the recognition of the narrowness of the measures in the AAT had led to the use of an additional, district-level, 'toolkit' for measuring Adviser performance. This toolkit measures a much wider range of input behaviour such as referrals to DMA, referrals to different types of provision, establishment of a Jobseeker's Agreement (JSAg) and also 'other appropriate action'. This was felt by respondents in and above this district, to provide a more appropriate balance of information on which to judge Adviser performance. Because of its breadth, the toolkit was thought to be more effective in highlighting training needs by identifying where an Adviser could have done more with a client in their WFI.

The perceived rigidity of the AAT model was also highlighted in discussions with Advisers about the use of BOCs. The AAT dictates that these should be routinely carried out, the assumption being that clients require this information as part of the effort to persuade them about the benefits of the transition to work. However, Advisers reported that many clients have been through the system several times, have been in and out of work and are often thus well informed about how much better off they would be in work. In these cases it seemed rather mechanistic and functional to go through the process of a BOC.

Despite the general message about over-reliance on the submissions target in the AAT, it was widely reported that observations, casework and team meetings are used more intensively than previously to support Adviser performance than under JET. The change to JOT was regarded as making such qualitative methods more appropriate and effective, especially through the increased willingness of Advisers to assist one another by sharing information and experience. The general impact of JOT had been to focus attention on a broader and more balanced use of performance data, drawing on both qualitative and quantitative evidence. However, it was also reported that observations in particular are not always conducted as often as they should be due to time and resource pressures, which helps to reinforce the reliance on less qualitative methods like the AAT.

Interestingly, in discussions with respondents about what sort of interventions and monitoring worked in supporting Advisers to increase their performance, it was reported that coaching, encouragement and qualitative supervision through the use of structured observations of Adviser interviews (using the QAF) worked, especially when used in conjunction with more quantitative data, produced, for instance, through the AAT. However, the use of qualitative methods is often more difficult and time consuming for managers than simply relying on outcome data (as under JET) or input data (as under JOT, with the AAT), meaning that these are often overused. Interestingly, the fieldwork revealed little evidence of use of the wider set of KMIs. The message from the evaluation appears to be the need to stress that the balanced use of the full range of available performance management tools, including the AAT, KMIs and observations is the most effective way of managing performance under JOT.

3.6.3   Self-monitoring of performance

An additional key finding from the initial evaluation was that staff themselves were uncertain about how their future performance would be measured and how they could prove that they were working effectively. Advisers in particular were, thus, keeping personal records of their own performance as means of protecting themselves from any future request to prove their effectiveness. The follow-on evaluation found that staff still retain personal records of performance, including not only evidence of job entries but also of comments from clients and employers about their performance at work. Staff retain this information in a variety of ways, including computer and paper records. There was some disagreement between different Adviser and Business Managers about the extent to which such information can be used as legitimate evidence of performance in monthly one-to-one and annual appraisal meetings. The findings suggest that there continues to be some confusion about the type of evidence that Advisers and frontline staff are to record about their own performance and exactly how this is to be used within the appraisal system.

Respondents also continued to report that they saw more timely and widely available district-level performance data and assessments as beneficial. There were concerns in some districts that this information was not communicated to all levels of staff and some felt that doing so would help them to better understand their own contribution to overall district-level performance.

3.6.4   Capacity to manage individuals and groups

A key finding from the initial evaluation was that some managers were still uncertain about their capacity to manage the performance of individual and groups of staff. The shift from JET to JOT involved a major shift in organisational culture and emphasis within Jobcentre Plus. The JET regime was deeply embedded in the organisational culture – the shared views and values among staff in the organisation. Managers and Advisers previously relied heavily on the availability of timely and outcome-based performance data available down to individual level. As such, it is to be expected that the shift to the types of performance management required under JOT would take time to settle down.

The follow-on evaluation offers the opportunity to assess the extent to which this settling process has taken place. Discussions with Adviser and Business Managers and also District Manager respondents revealed a continuing variation of views and comfort with their capacity to manage individual and group performance. On one hand, a variety of respondents suggested that the previous performance management system had been overly narrow in scope. The emphasis on input data ushered in by JOT was felt by this group of respondents to allow a more balanced consideration of performance using the range of performance data available from the AAT, observations of Adviser interviews, case conferences and one-to-ones.

Others continued to be less comfortable with the overall performance management arrangements. These respondents suggested that they continued to feel that there was a less pronounced emphasis on performance as a result of the loss of Daily Placing List and timely outcome performance data. The loss of this data was thought to distract from the focus on motivation and immediate identification of problems, making performance management more difficult.

3.7   Staff and organisational capacity

A key finding of the initial evaluation of the JOT Pilots was that JOT required a significant change in emphasis within the organisation and that many staff would need to augment their skills sets to cope with the change. Advisers need to be more aware of the range of non-contract provision available and techniques and measures that work in supporting the hardest-to-help customer groups to move closer to the labour market. Adviser Managers need to be better able to use a variety of performance measures, including observations, case conferencing and one-to-ones to support Advisers through sharing information and good practice and offering coaching-style support to adapt to the types of behaviour required under JOT. For Business and District Managers there was a need to understand the range of input performance management information available and to develop techniques to support Adviser Managers in their role. Generally, there is a need to shift to a more qualitative and supportive style of management from a numbers-based and directive style of management. The initial evaluation also reported that more senior levels of the Jobcentre Plus and Department for Work and Pensions hierarchy would also need to be aware of the need for caution and circumspection when interpreting short-term performance trends.

As Section 3.2 demonstrates, a number of changes have impacted on the ability of the case study districts to develop these types of skills and therefore, to build appropriate organisational capacity. Principal among these have been ongoing changes to the workforce, both through headcount reduction and the restructuring of staff grades, especially for Adviser Managers. This latter change has meant that some of the investment in Adviser Manager capacity has been lost and that an even more dramatic cultural shift is required of the staff that are now filling the more senior Adviser Manager positions.

Regardless of whether these workforce changes are responsible, the follow-on evaluation suggests that there is a continued need to build the capacity of the organisation to fully utilise the range of sources of performance information available and how these can be used to interpret individual level performance. There is also a need to ensure that the appropriate staff have the skills necessary to coach and support high performance and improvement.

3.8   Customer service

Overall, the level and quality of service reported by Jobcentre Plus customers did not appear to have changed significantly as a result of the introduction of JOT. However, making qualitative judgements on these issues is complicated by differing perspectives on what a good quality service from Jobcentre Plus would be. For instance, some customers dislike the emphasis on work first which is at the heart of the Welfare to Work Strategy and thus, see it as poor quality service when this is reflected in their interaction with Jobcentre Plus. On the other hand, others see assistance in finding suitable work or training as good quality service.

There was little consensus among customers from PG1, PG2 and PG3 about the level of one-to-one support and Adviser time that they have received since the introduction of JOT. Some clearly reported that they had experienced improvements in the amount of Adviser time they received and reported on this positively. Where this was the case, there was some evidence that customers were now able to enjoy a more effective relationship with their Adviser, for instance through greater continuity:

> *'I find I can discuss issues with my* [Personal Adviser] *now as we are more familiar with each other.'*

(PG2 customer)

> *'I get to see the same member of staff every time I sign which is better.'*

(PG2 customer)

Others reported that they had noticed an increased emphasis on work in their contact with Jobcentre Plus staff. In some cases this was positively received as improving the support received for job search:

> *'The improvements have come from the fact that the Jobcentre now selects and sends me application forms for jobs that I probably wouldn't have found myself using the Jobpoints.'*

(PG2 customer)

> *'I have had a few calls at home from my PA with information about vacancies she thought would suit me...and this wasn't something I'd had before.'*

(PG3 customer)

In other cases, this increased work-first emphasis was not always positively received, either because respondents did not feel that they were able to work because their barriers to employment had not been overcome or because they felt that Jobcentre Plus was not able to provide, directly or indirectly, access to the support that they needed to move into work. In particular, where this was in relation to the quality of vacancies that they were able to access, with these being frequently perceived as of poor quality, low skilled, low paid or in the 'wrong' geographical location:

'Advisers now only seem to discuss the jobs that they want you to do…not the ones that you want to do.'

(PG2 customer)

'They assume that you'll take any old job.'

(PG2 customer)

'We are getting told to go for jobs we don't want to do like cleaning and bar work.'

(PG2 customer)

However, neither the perception that Jobcentre Plus was becoming more work-first or that the hardest-to-help customers were getting increased adviser time were universal. For instance, other client respondents from PG1 and PG2 reported that they did not perceive the amount of time they spend with their adviser to have increased. Some reported that this had decreased.

In line with the drive of the Welfare to Work Strategy, customers from Priority Groupsdid appear to be referred to self-help channels. This is discussed in more detail in Section 4.4. Where these customers had received some help with job search activity, they did not appear to have noticed any difference in the quality of this.

In general, it was difficult to attribute any of the changes in the perception of customers to the influence of JOT on staff behaviour. Indeed it was difficult to identify any clear pattern across the different customer groups or the sample as a whole, in relation to perceived changes in the quality of service on the part of customers. Customer perceptions appeared to be highly dependent on the individual's own experiences rather than determined by broader patterns in service delivery. Despite this, the research did not identify any evidence to suggest that JOT had resulted in a change in the overall quality of service from Jobcentre Plus in ways which would impact negatively on the achievement of the wider Welfare to Work agenda.

3.9   Key findings

The evidence from the follow-up study confirms the generally positive contribution of JOT to the Welfare to Work Strategy. JOT itself is associated with driving behaviours which are consistent with helping the hardest-to-help customers move closer to the labour market, overcome their barriers to work and move into sustainable employment. However, the implementation of JOT has been impacted on by a number of contextual changes within the organisation which may have made the transition to a new culture of performance management more challenging and in some cases may have also constrained the positive contribution of JOT.

These contextual factors include continued instability and uncertainty with regard to the size and organisation of the Jobcentre Plus workforce. These efficiency related changes have been augmented by changes to the organisation of the workforce, particularly in relation to Adviser Managers. This is particularly important as Adviser Managers are a key group of staff under JOT and bear the majority of the responsibility for implementing new performance management procedures, such as the use of qualitative observations, coaching and individual support. The wider implications of efficiency initiatives and changes in the orientation of the organisation, such as declining levels of formal contracted provision, have also constrained the capacity of Jobcentre Plus offices to make the successful transition to the types of working practices which JOT requires and encourages.

A more complex contextual factor for JOT is the increasing focus on work-first as part of the wider Welfare to Work strategy. While JOT is potentially well aligned with this message, much depends on how it is interpreted in terms of the types of behaviour expected of individual staff and in relation to individual customers. There was some evidence that the combination of this, rising JSA registers and the introduction of the AAT was beginning to confuse the interpretation of the linkages between JOT and Welfare to Work among many staff.

The awareness and understanding among staff of JOT was generally good. However, a number of uncertainties remained. Staff did in places, still worry that they did not fully understand the linkages between their own performance and the performance of Jobcentre Plus as a whole. This was due to the loss of direct individual outcome performance data but conversely, most respondents did understand the assumed linkages between appropriate advice, submissions and referrals and the achievement of positive job outcomes. This lack of understanding, therefore, may be more due to the transition to a new culture in which links between individual workplace behaviour and outcome performance are more implicit and assumed than explicit and direct, rather than a lack of understanding of JOT itself.

One area where confusion did appear to be important, however, was in relation to the types of advice, referrals and submissions that are driven by the performance management regime. The transition to JOT was widely perceived as a transition to helping the most disadvantaged customers and that this would often involve a shift away from a volume-first submissions policy. It was widely reported that more sophisticated submissions and referrals behaviour had been driven by JOT and the removal of the pressure to generate quick job entries. However, the introduction of the AAT had clearly confused this message and some respondents at district and office management levels as well as Advisers reported that submissions behaviour may revert or had already reverted to a more JET-like approach of generating a high volume of submissions in the hope that some of these would result in a job outcome. There was also widespread dissatisfaction and frustration with this, and a widely reported feeling that such a change would be regressive and to some extent, in conflict with the objective of helping the hardest-to-help customers move into sustainable work.

An additional area where the impact of JOT-related working practices may have a negative impact on Welfare to Work was in relation to follow-up of submissions activity. Because Advisers were no longer routinely following-up submissions to employers, they had less information on which to base their advice to customers and to identify those customers who were not actively seeking work. However, it may be that less pressure to undertake follow-up in every case makes such information gathering more deliberate and targeted as Advisers did suggest that they still undertook follow-up, either where they thought there may be benefit to the customer in seeking employer feedback on applications and interview performance or where they suspected an individual was not actively seeking work.

More encouraging evidence was found in relation to the use of financial support to customers in making the transition to work and to team working within Jobcentre Plus offices. ADF use had fallen dramatically and was widely thought to be used in a much more appropriate fashion. It was also widely reported that conflict and tension between staff in Jobcentre Plus offices had fallen as a result of the introduction of JOT and removal of individual competition for points. This had had the knock-on implication that staff were more willing to work together and share skills, knowledge and experience to help customers.

The transition to JOT emphasises the need to use a wider range of more complex information in managing individual performance. While there was evidence that this transition was underway, the introduction of the AAT in particular, had disrupted this and there was some evidence of a transition back to reliance on a narrower range of headline data. Preventing this from becoming embedded will be a key challenge for managing the change in organisational culture required by JOT.

These key findings suggest that there is a need for organisational and institutional stability to implement the Welfare to Work agenda. This relates to staffing, organisational changes and also clarity and consistency in the messages about appropriate staff behaviour and organisational culture which emanates from official guidance and the performance management system. It is important to bear in mind that Jobcentre Plus has a deeply embedded organisational and cultural commitment to the use of performance indicators and within the organisation there is a marked tendency to utilise simplistic headline measures, regardless of widely held concerns about their quality. As such, additional care needs to be taken to ensure that performance management tools, like the AAT, are used appropriately and are accompanied by guidance which makes clear that a balanced approach to measuring individual and team performance is most effective and that under JOT, qualitative performance management is at least as important as the use of quantitative headline data.

4 Support for the Jobcentre Plus Channels Strategy

4.1 Key elements of the Channels Strategy

The Jobcentre Plus Channels Strategy sets out the objectives of the organisation in terms of making the most efficient and effective possible use of the various job search channels that are available to Jobcentre Plus customers[1], notably:

- Jobpoint terminals;

- Jobseeker Direct;

- Apply Direct;

- the Jobcentre Plus website;

- non-Jobcentre Plus channels, where appropriate.

In particular, the strategy presents an aspiration that, as far as possible, customers that are able to use these 'self-help' channels without the intervention of Jobcentre Plus staff should be encouraged and facilitated to do so. To the extent that this strategy is successful, it is anticipated that staff resources should be diverted towards providing more intensive support for those that need it and are most likely to benefit in terms of moving towards the labour market. Clearly, this strategy is consistent with and linked with the wider Welfare to Work Strategy discussed in Chapter 3.

---

[1] The Channels Strategy is concerned with both employers and individual customers. Employers as customers are discussed in Chapter 5; this chapter focuses on individual customers.

The design of the Job Outcome Target (JOT) is consistent with the Channels Strategy in a number of ways:

- The primary focus of JOT is upon customers that move from benefits into work, providing an incentive for the concentration of resources on longer-term benefit claimants and other high priority groups (such as lone parents) rather than short-term claimants, non-claimants and people who are already in work. Early findings from the JOT Pilot qualitative evaluation suggested that, under the Job Entry Target (JET), some offices were investing significant resources in initiatives to place large volumes of non-claimants (e.g. students) into – typically – part-time and/or temporary jobs. Under JOT, incentives for Jobcentre Plus to undertake such activities are limited.

- Under JOT, job outcomes achieved through Jobseeker Direct, Apply Direct and the Jobcentre Plus website – and indeed through channels outside the Jobcentre Plus system – are attributed to the Jobcentre Plus district in which the customer lives, providing that the customer is claiming some type of benefit. For non-claimants, job outcomes only count towards the district's target in certain cases (e.g. Jobseeker Direct) in which an LMS record has been created. Again, this provides an incentive for Jobcentre Plus staff to encourage 'work ready' individuals to use self-help channels without fear of 'losing' the job outcome.

- Following on from the above, JOT represents a significant move away from individual performance measures and targets towards a district-level approach, thus reducing the incentive for individual members of staff to concentrate on assisting 'job ready' customers in order to ensure that the resulting job entry points are assigned to them personally.

The qualitative and quantitative evaluations of the JOT Pilots suggested that the above factors were indeed having an impact, with signs of significant shifts in attitude and behaviour on the part of 'frontline' staff in particular and changes in the organisation of frontline services, notably the increasing profile of 'floorwalkers' and similar groups of staff.

On the other hand, concerns were expressed by some Jobcentre Plus staff that the increasing emphasis upon self-help channels may be perceived negatively by customers, an assertion that was not corroborated through qualitative interviews with customers. Doubts were also expressed about the quality of service provided through – for example – Jobpoints and Jobseeker Direct, while other Jobcentre Plus respondents felt that some customers would find it difficult to use telephone and particularly computer-based services.

Difficulties with accessing the self-help channels was not thought to be limited to the hardest-to-help customers, with some staff reporting that they felt that even job-ready customers often struggle. For these reasons – together with limited confidence about their own ability to identify 'job ready' customers – some Jobcentre Plus respondents felt uncomfortable about the shift of focus towards self-help channels.

Finally, the Pilot evaluations highlighted the fact that JOT was only one of a range of factors driving or supporting the shift towards the use of self-help channels by job-ready customers. Pressures on staff numbers, the 'Footfall Project' and various Pilot programmes designed to streamline the new claims and FJR processes all played a role and there was also some feeling that customers were becoming more competent and confident with the new technology. Indeed, our customer consultations found that some customers prefer to use self-help channels rather than to interact with Jobcentre Plus staff.

This report updates the above findings and investigates the extent to which the trends identified in the Pilot evaluations have continued as the JOT initiative has become more established in the Option 1 Pilot districts.

4.2   Contextual changes

As noted already, a number of changes took place since the previous JOT qualitative evaluation exercise in summer 2005 that have implications for the Channels Strategy and the role of JOT in supporting it. These include:

- The **Footfall Project**, which is designed to reduce footfall within Jobcentre Plus offices, particularly among job-ready customers in PG4 and PG5. This reflects primarily a desire to optimise the use of physical and human resources within a context of pressures to reduce headcount and office space and focus resources on higher Priority Groups to support the Welfare to Work agenda. Given this, it might be expected that – even in the absence of JOT – some customers would be discouraged from making visits to Jobcentre Plus offices and encouraged to use self-help channels from their own telephones or computers.

- Initiatives designed to optimise the use of staff resources and encourage frontline staff to distinguish at an early stage between **new claimants and short-term unemployed customers** who are able to use self-help channels from those who might benefit from more intensive support from Jobcentre Plus staff. Again, regardless of the introduction of JOT, it might be expected that this process would lead to greater use of self-help channels.

- The **Organisational Design Review (ODR)** led, in the period immediately prior to the follow-on study fieldwork, to the actual or planned closure or merger of a number of Jobcentre Plus offices in the Pilot districts. This, again, might be expected to encourage some customers, particularly those in more remote locations, to use self-help channels rather than travelling to Jobcentre Plus offices.

- More generally, the overall context of **resource and headcount reductions** across Jobcentre Plus, led many offices to examine the types of frontline services provided, with the Response to Displayed Vacancies (RDV) service coming under particular scrutiny. Such services have been reduced or withdrawn in many offices over a number of months, further reinforcing the trend towards encouraging customers to 'help themselves'.

- A further factor noted by some Jobcentre Plus respondents concerns **the changing nature of PG4 and PG5 customers**, and in particular the increasing number of economic migrant workers from the EU Accession States who are utilising Jobcentre Plus services. This trend is contradictory to the others outlined above in that it tends to mean that relatively more resource needs to be deployed to help customers who have a limited command of English and may not be familiar with the UK labour market.

- Finally, as suggested above, changes in **customer attitudes and abilities** may be partially responsible for increases in the use of self-help channels, with the internet in particular becoming a tool that is increasingly used by job seekers in general, and not just by those seeking managerial and professional jobs.

This discussion suggests that JOT is only one of a whole range of factors that might potentially drive a shift towards the use of self-help channels by some groups of Jobcentre Plus customers. This conclusion is reflected in the comments of Jobcentre Plus managers and staff, the vast majority of who stated that there had been a clear and significant shift towards the use of self-help channels since the introduction of the JOT Pilot in January 2005. No respondents felt that JOT was solely or even primarily responsible for such a shift, but all respondents that discussed the issue were clear that JOT was consistent with, and supportive of, this general trend.

4.3   Jobcentre Plus staff behaviour and attitudes

An important finding emerging from the follow-on study in relation to behaviour and attitudes of staff towards the increasing use of self-help channels is a general (but not universal) perception of some improvements in the quality of services provided by self-help channels, notably the Jobpoints, Jobseeker Direct and the Jobcentre Plus website. While there were still concerns regarding, for example, the accuracy of the information contained on the Jobpoints (echoed by some customers – see below) the overall picture seems to be one of gradually improving service levels. This appears to have increased the confidence of some frontline staff members to encourage customers to use self-help channels where they may have been reluctant to do so in the past.

Most Jobcentre Plus respondents were clear that the design of JOT, and its implementation is supportive of the Channels Strategy. While JOT was not the primary factor behind increasing use of self-help channels, in general it was felt that JOT has played an important role.

Earlier JOT qualitative evaluation studies revealed that some frontline staff in particular felt uncomfortable about the prospect of encouraging customers to use self-help channels. There were two main aspects to this: Firstly, some staff members felt that they did not have the skills or resources to enable them to distinguish between 'job ready' customers and those in need of further support. Secondly, there was a general feeling that customers expect and prefer face-to-face contact and encouraging the use of self-help channels represented inferior customer service.

'Self-help channels don't always work as they should. For example, a recent local area search on job points threw up jobs in Nottingham and London. Also, customers are not always comfortable with self-help channels – although this is improving.'

Adviser Manager

'Referring job-ready clients to self-help channels generally works but there can be difficulties accessing 'warm phones' because of customers making calls to the Social Fund. Increased self-help also makes it difficult to check whether customers are actively seeking work.'

Adviser Manager

The follow-on research encountered both of these issues in the responses of some of the frontline staff members interviewed. However, the overall picture was one of increasing confidence in the strategy and a general sense that encouraging the use of self-help channels did not necessary represent inferior customer service.

Managers and staff interviewed for the follow-on study described further moves towards the effective deployment of floorwalkers and the provision of assistance for customers who might be struggling, for example, with the Jobpoint terminals. Again, this did not necessarily result directly from JOT, but was seen as consistent with an overall strategy to focus resources more effectively on those that need advisory support while continuing to provide a universal free service for all customers who wish to undertake job search activities.

One contradictory trend, already noted in Chapter 3, relates to the submission targets contained within the AAT model. Some respondents felt that these targets provided an incentive for Advisers to undertake submissions for customers who are willing and able to undertake their own job search activity. No concrete examples of this occurring were, however, provided.

It is clear from the evidence of the follow-on study that JOT has continued to play a supporting role in ensuring that frontline staff and Advisers do not have an incentive to undertake interventions with customers who are willing and able to utilise the various self-help channels that are available to them. In general, the 'JOT effect' has been reinforced by a range of initiatives and activities around the use of floorwalkers and the refocusing of the efforts of frontline staff away from RDV and related activities towards more intensive Jobseeker's Allowance (JSA) interventions.

Perceived improvements in the quality of some of the services provided have also supported this process, although Jobcentre Plus staff that were interviewed identified a number of further potential improvements, notably around better information on the Jobpoints and improved availability and management of the use of 'warm phones'.

4.4   Customer experiences and attitudes

Evidence from focus groups with 110 PGs1-3 customers and interviews with 124 customers in the PG4 and PG5 groups in general supports the findings from Jobcentre Plus staff interviews, in that the vast majority of respondents stated that they had used some form of self-help channel in their recent job search activities. Indeed customers across all groups had noticed some increase in the extent to which they were referred to self-service channels. This is particularly the case among PGs1-3 customers, while it is more difficult to discern a trend among non-claimants who tended not to have used Jobcentre Plus over a long period of time.

Customers revealed almost no awareness of JOT or Jobcentre Plus targets in general, so it is difficult to assess the extent to which customers' experiences were driven primarily by changes in the target regime. However, it is possible to state that customers' responses are consistent with the changes anticipated as a result of JOT.

The majority of customers stated that they felt comfortable with using self-help channels, with some valuing the privacy and flexibility of making contact with employers from home. PG1-3 customers, in particular, emphasised the need for this to go hand-in-hand with personal contact and guidance. Again, this is consistent with JOT, in that Advisers should not have an incentive to try to ensure that 'their' customers are submitted by the Adviser to a job opportunity. As long as the customer succeeds in entering employment, the credit for the achievement will go to the district as a whole. Under JET, performance points may have been 'claimed' by other Jobcentre Plus colleagues or indeed not credited to the organisation at all.

Nonetheless, customers reported some difficulties with the use of self-help channels that were inhibiting the benefit that they might gain from using them and in some cases, lead the respondent to be dissatisfied with the service received from Jobcentre Plus. In particular, the variable quality of information contained on the Jobpoints was a common cause for concern:

> *'Remove unavailable jobs displayed on the Jobpoints. Jobcentre Plus should do regular checks with employers to make sure vacancies still exist. It's a time-consuming and frustrating process.'*

(PG4/5 customer)

> *'Jobpoints should be more accurate. You can put in Huddersfield jobs and they bring up Newcastle.'*

(PG4/5 customer)

> *'The Jobpoints are not updated on a regular basis so when you enquire about a job you find it has been taken. When you search for local jobs in London it displays some located in Scotland. You ask it to search for part-time work and it comes up with full-time work. Take a serious look at this.'*

(PG4/5 customer)

The frequent need to queue for the warm phones (for those unable or unwilling to use their own telephone) was a further cause for concern.

The general picture, however, among customers across all groups was one of broad satisfaction with services received, with little change in satisfaction levels over time[2]. In general, the customers who felt that they would like more face-to-face contact were balanced by those that felt comfortable with the current situation and indeed would be happy to make more use of self-help channels. Similarly, some respondents felt that it was harder to talk to staff about vacancies than previously, but an equal number stated that more staff were available and/or that it is 'easier to talk' to staff about vacancies:

> *'Jobseeker Direct are very helpful and pleasant...they make you feel like a customer.'*

(PG3 customer)

> *'I personally find them very helpful...the person I go and see...she always asks me what I'm doing to find work...she says hopefully I won't need to see you in two weeks...she always says that when I leave.'*

(PG3 customer)

> *'I find that I can discuss most issues with my PA now as we are more familiar with each other.'*

(PG2 customer)

It is clear from this brief overview of customer views and experiences that JOT has not directly affected customer perceptions of service, but has indirectly supported a shift toward self-help channels that has been recognised by many customers and does not appear to have had a significant impact on their views of the service. Indeed, the fact that the majority of the changes in service noted by customers had no connection with JOT, suggests that it has played a relatively minor role in the eyes of customers.

It is also clear that improvements in the information contained on the Jobpoints, the increased availability of 'help desk' type staff and actions to increase the accessibility of warm phones would further enhance a process that appears to be well entrenched and entirely consistent with the aims of JOT and the Channels Strategy.

---

[2] Note the qualitative nature of the study and the difficulties involved in assessing change over time for infrequent or one-off users of Jobcentre Plus services.

4.5   Key findings

The evidence from the qualitative follow-on study of the JOT Option 1 districts confirms the supportive role played by JOT in relation to the Jobcentre Plus Channels Strategy. Indeed, the follow-on study provides indications that this supportive role may strengthen as the behaviour and culture associated with JOT become more embedded over time. The majority of Jobcentre Plus staff in the Pilot districts are no longer concerned primarily with individual performance targets, as was the case under JET, resulting in a greater acceptance at all levels of the need to focus resources on 'harder to help' groups, with the outcome being the encouragement of 'job ready' customers to use self-help channels.

These attitudes and behaviour are most prevalent among frontline staff and are buttressed by a range of initiatives designed to reduce footfall, use resources more effectively and identify 'job-ready' individuals at an early stage. JOT also appears to have provided incentives to Advisers to encourage their clients to use a wider range of job search channels without fear of 'losing' any resulting job outcomes.

Feedback from customers suggests that they recognise the increasing trend towards the use of self-help channels, although they do not link it to changes in the Jobcentre Plus target regime. In general, customers are happy with this process, although some concerns were expressed about the quality of services provided through self-help channels. Some customers expressed a desire for more personal contact with Jobcentre Plus staff, but this was a minority view, with most customers suggesting that service quality had remained broadly constant over recent months.

The research identified a number of issues to be addressed in relation to ensuring that JOT continues to be consistent with, and play a supporting role in, the Jobcentre Plus Channels Strategy:

- There is widespread concern that the AAT submission target may undermine the contribution of JOT Channels Strategy by providing an incentive for Advisers to submit customers rather than encouraging them to use self-help channels where appropriate.

- The perceived quality of self-help channels plays an important role in the attitudes and behaviour of Jobcentre Plus staff and customers. The supporting role of JOT would be enhanced by improvements in key areas, notably the timeliness and accuracy of vacancy information on Jobpoints, the accessibility of warm phones and the availability of staff to provide assistance to customers who require it.

- Following on from the above, the qualitative findings suggest that the impact of JOT on the use of self-help channels is felt most strongly where the role of floorwalkers has been enhanced to provide not only a 'signposting' service but also an element of customer service and support.

- Greater understanding of the behaviour and attitudes of customers in relation to the use of self-help channels would help to reassure those members of staff who are still concerned about the customer service implications of JOT and the Channels Strategy. This would also help to identify areas for improvement that should make JOT more effective in encouraging the most effective possible use of resources to support job seekers.

5 Support for employer engagement and relationships with providers

5.1 Impact of JOT on relationships with employers

5.1.1 The views of Jobcentre Plus staff

The majority of Jobcentre Plus staff interviewed expressed the view that the Job Outcome Target (JOT) has replaced the previous pervading emphasis on volume submissions to jobs. Instead, JOT is seen to have fostered an approach to submissions more shaped by customers' own aspirations and the requirements of employers. Staff were also sure, in the main, that JOT provides a real opportunity to form better relationships with employers as a result of far fewer blanket submissions and more job-matching activity.

> *'There is not that quick-fix mentality anymore. Now we look at job sustainability for the customer and whether they are the employee that the employer really wants.'*

(Jobcentre Plus Adviser)

A number of respondents mentioned small and medium sized enterprises (SMEs) in particular and how they must welcome the fewer and more appropriate submissions, coupled with the lower level of administrative contact they now receive. Some staff mentioned that large employers in their districts continue to provide 'follow-up lists' that are actioned to ensure good practice in the relationship between larger firms and Jobcentre Plus. However, there is far less follow-up in general. Employers are still contacted but this now tends to be specific to an individual customer – for example, to brief the employer on the customer's needs, or to check on feedback to help a customer's interview skills – and is no longer simply about 'chasing numbers'. Indeed, a number of staff mentioned they are happy that they no longer have to explain to employers the vagaries of the previous internal Jobcentre Plus points system.

'I used to be embarrassed ringing up employers chasing job entries; they don't want to be messing around with that.'

(Jobcentre Plus Adviser)

However, some frontline advisers mentioned that their relationship with employers has actually become less pronounced and that the balance in their relationship with customer and employer has moved closer to the customer. Some advisers reported that they have significantly less contact with employers now and several spoke of a recent move away from large-scale recruitment events and job fairs in their districts.

Several team leaders and managers also mentioned that although employers can see the efforts that Jobcentre Plus are making in relation to targeted submissions, there is a need to concentrate more on adviser contact with employers – both prior to and after the submission process. This will not only improve the information flow about customers to employers but will also help to gain information about a customer's performance at a job interview.

Indeed, several Team Leaders and Managers stated that JOT has revealed certain areas where employer engagement in general needs to be improved. For example, one Deputy District Manager reported some problems with their Employer Outcome Target performance. Employers are now having their vacancies automatically closed without follow-up by Jobcentre Plus offices. And this drop-off in employer contact has resulted in an abrupt end to the continuity that many employers within the district had come to appreciate. Feedback on this issue to the Regional Performance Manager has now resulted in an instruction being cascaded to VSMs that they must inform employers that their vacancies will be automatically closed.

However, despite their low Employer Outcome scores, this district has seen its score for overall employer satisfaction rise to 90 per cent. It appears to the district that it is the matching element of the Employer Outcome Target that is the issue and this is now being examined.

Furthermore, several respondents from across the districts sampled stated that they feel JOT has also indirectly encouraged greater emphasis on the role of Labour Market Intelligence. In order to ensure appropriate and timely submissions, many staff are finding that they need to be more aware of developments in their local labour markets: for example, what notified vacancies their office has received, what job advertisements are appearing in local newspapers, which employers are recruiting, and which employers are making redundancies. Developments like these are viewed as important tenets in the new logic of 'appropriate action'.

5.1.2 The views of employers

For those employers interviewed, there were a range of different experiences and views. However, given the relatively small sample size, the responses should be taken as indicative rather than representative. While it is difficult to directly attribute the changes identified to the impact of JOT, it is likely that it has helped to drive these.

Of the 24 employers interviewed, five reported no obvious change or fluctuation in their relationship with Jobcentre Plus. One did, however, express concern about the end of their previous good relationship with the local office. The employer explained that contact had declined steadily over several months until they were informed by Jobcentre Plus that they would no longer have a designated contact at all. The employer stated that they had come to rely on Jobcentre Plus to service their vacancies and felt 'dumped'.

The disappointment of the removal of designated contacts at Jobcentre Plus was also shared by two other employers, who both stated that this effectively removed a sense of partnership in their dealings with Jobcentre Plus. Comments on this aspect included two examples of employers having to chase their local Jobcentre Plus for information on the progression of vacancies.

The employers were, however, generally pleased with the service they receive from Jobcentre Plus. Evidence from a small number of employers appeared to support the argument that JOT has led to an increased quality in submissions procedures with employers commenting on a smaller number of applicants and an increase in their quality. One employer mentioned that a recent recruitment led to the drawing up of a waiting list of suitable candidates – something that has never happened before with Jobcentre Plus referrals.

Evidence from employers also corroborated that gained through work with Jobcentre Plus staff in relation to a decline in the amount of staff time spent on employer follow-up. Where employers had noticed any difference in their relationship with Jobcentre Plus, they tended to report less frequent contact with the local office and a lower level of detailed follow-up of individual submissions. At the same time, employers also reported a higher level of courtesy-type calls from Employer Direct to check on progress with vacancies. While this was generally welcomed by employers, many also regretted the consequential loss of contact with the local office and in some cases, employers had concerns about the resource demands of placing vacancies with Employer Direct.

Some other employer comments are also worth mentioning. Notably, the view of one that successive designated contacts at Jobcentre Plus have lacked appropriate sectoral knowledge. Another employer mentioned that they had seen a noticeable rise in the number of Jobcentre Plus applicants who had been referred as 'job ready' but who had made fundamental mistakes when filling in the application form. Nevertheless, only one employer interviewed stated that they would not use Jobcentre Plus again.

Also, only one employer reported some knowledge of Jobcentre Plus target systems – and then only from what they had learned informally from their designated contact.

5.2   Impact of JOT on relationships with providers

5.2.1   The views of Jobcentre Plus staff

A major benefit of JOT in relation to provision that was highlighted by a number of Jobcentre Plus staff has been the removal of pressure to automatically submit harder-to-help customers. JOT is seen to have provided increased scope for interventions to address barriers to work over a longer period of time. And this increased scope for interventions has dovetailed to some extent with the rise in the use of non-contracted provision over recent months. At the same time, it has generated some concerns about the range of non-contracted provision available and the quality of that currently on offer.

Most of the comments made by Jobcentre Plus staff about the use of provision related to the range and quality of provision available. While JOT may have impacted on the use of provision, most of the comments and responses received referred to contracting arrangements with providers rather than JOT. The one issue that JOT did appear to have impacted on was the willingness of staff to first look for the type of support that might be the most suitable for a client and to refer to that provision rather than submitting them to a job immediately. This willingness was not perceived as a decline in the commitment to Welfare to Work, but more a commitment to more sustainable job entries.

Most of the comments of Jobcentre Plus staff about their use of provision related to the reduction in the amount available:

> 'It means that we can't help these people at the most important time – when they first sign on. A lot of our young customers need basic skills training or ESOL.'

(Jobcentre Plus Adviser)

While this was clearly an important issue and generated some degree of frustration it was not driven by JOT but by the wider contracting arrangements between providers and Jobcentre Plus. Where it is relevant to JOT is in restricting the options available to Advisers in helping the hardest-to-help to move closer to the labour market.

5.2.2   The views of providers

Whilst mindful of the fact that a small sample of providers was selected for this follow-up study, several points of interest can be identified. Services provided by the providers interviewed included:

- forklift truck training;
- wage-subsidised training at a manufacturer of wood products;
- workplace training and recruitment for arts and culture organisations;

- over-50s job clubs;
- basic skills, self-employment and IT training;
- construction training;
- skills for life training;
- training and employability support for those with drug dependencies;
- work-related support for those recently made redundant;
- New Deal for Disabled People training;
- New Deal mentoring service.

In respect of those non-contracted providers interviewed, none had experienced a large increase in Jobcentre Plus referrals over recent months. But this may simply be due to the small number of providers in the sample. They did, however, refer to the fact that it tends to be the same Jobcentre Plus Advisers who make all the referrals. This is despite regular and ongoing attempts by providers to promote their services to all Jobcentre Plus staff. Interviews with Jobcentre Plus staff contradicted this to an extent – suggesting that they were all now looking to make referrals to a broader range of provision.

One non-contracted provider mentioned that they had previously been able to visit their local Jobcentre Plus offices whenever necessary in order to promote their services and engage with customers. Now, Jobcentre Plus have restricted these visits to designated times and the provider believes that this has impacted negatively on the number of Jobcentre Plus referrals. Moreover, since they are now far more reliant on referrals being made by Jobcentre Plus Advisers, the provider has noticed that many more clients are getting 'lost' between the Jobcentre Plus referral and registration on the provision programme.

The seeming lack of communication between Jobcentre Plus Advisers and general lack of knowledge about the provider's service were cited by all the non-contracted providers. Two of those interviewed received the bulk of their funding from Learn Direct and yet despite having arranged several promotion events with their local Jobcentre Plus, they remained frustrated at the relatively low numbers of referrals. One of the Learn Direct-funded providers offers basic skills training and stated that they could easily accommodate double the current referrals from Jobcentre Plus. Being aware of recent reductions in provision resource at Jobcentre Plus, this provider has been promoting the fact that a referral to their services from Jobcentre Plus does not require Jobcentre Plus to draw upon their provision resource at all. However, referrals remain low.

Most of the contracted providers interviewed reported a tangible drop in Jobcentre Plus referrals over recent months, though this was more likely to be related to factors other than JOT.

5.3   Key findings

The shift towards 'appropriate action' to better facilitate customer needs and aspirations, supported by the developing practice of making targeted submissions to employers through better job-matching and improved LMI, was welcomed by all those Jobcentre Plus staff interviewed.

It appears that as many advisers now feel much less pressure to constantly reflect upon, and monitor, their own personal performance, they have begun to consider how their role fits within the new working culture that JOT has ushered in. The comments and views concerning how they might improve upon their customer service – in relation to targeted submissions, referrals to appropriate provision, and better LMI – all point to an ongoing process of JOT becoming more embedded in the day-to-day workings of teams and individual advisers.

The ongoing process of JOT becoming embedded across the roles and responsibilities of Jobcentre Plus staff is, to some extent, reflected in the comments and perspectives of those employers and providers interviewed. Although, as mentioned, the relatively small sample sizes of employers and providers interviewed for this follow-up report suggest that further investigation into employer and provider experiences would be of value.

Furthermore, the reduction in provision resource that occurred in parallel with JOT, but not as part of its overall design, can be seen to have resulted in some confusion and misunderstandings among Jobcentre Plus staff, employers, and providers alike. Continued efforts to better inform all parties of the context of changes in recent working practices would help rectify these misunderstandings and ease concerns.

Other issues that arose in relation to the relationship between Jobcentre Plus staff, employers and providers:

- As the balance in the relationship between advisers, customers and employers has moved towards the customer, a need has emerged among some teams to ensure that adviser/employer contact does not ebb too far.

- Employers noted the general decline in detailed follow-up of individual submissions from local officers but also noted an increased amount of courtesy-call activity from Employer Direct.

- A number of employers interviewed regretted the removal of designated contacts at their local Jobcentre Plus, and mentioned a general sense of less 'personal' service. A need to ensure the maintenance of both established and developing partnerships between Jobcentre Plus and employers is suggested here.

- Jobcentre Plus staff appeared to be more willing to make use of the full range of provision available rather than relying on contracted provision only. This was partly driven by the impact of JOT, but was in the main related to contracting arrangements with providers. Where JOT had been influential was in increasing Advisers' demand for information about the full range of available local provision in attempting to access more appropriate and effective support for the hardest-to-help service users.

6 Key findings and implications

6.1 Overall: the contribution of JOT to the wider operation of Jobcentre Plus

Overall, the contribution of the Job Outcome Target (JOT) to the wider role and activities of Jobcentre Plus was thought to be positive. JOT supported changes in staff behaviour and motivation in relation to the hardest-to-help groups and prioritised appropriate messages about how these customers could be helped to move towards sustainable work. Advisers felt enabled by JOT to give more appropriate advice and to make more effective submissions to employers and referrals to external, often non-contracted, provision. JOT was also thought to support the changing mode of service delivery of Jobcentre Plus services and its impact on staff behaviour was thought to be consistent with the wider Jobcentre Plus Channels Strategy which emphasises the use of self-help channels for those customers who benefit most from these, while allowing staff to spend a greater proportion of their time with those customers who require face-to-face support. Evidence about the relationship with providers and employers was mixed. While employers had not noticed any significant deterioration in the quality of service delivery, some did lament a loss of direct contact with locally based Jobcentre Plus staff and staff themselves suggested that this might impair their ability to gather the types of information that can help customers move into work. The prominent feature in the relationship with providers was not JOT but declining levels of contracted provision.

However, the positive contribution of JOT after 18 months of operation, to the wider Welfare to Work and Channels Strategies, in particular, may have been undermined by workforce, organisational and institutional instability and by the introduction of the Adviser Achievement Tool (AAT) and the submissions target within it. This was thought to incentivise behaviours which were more consistent with the previous Job Entry Target (JET) regime, such as volume-submissions and working face-to-face with customers who are able to use self-service channels effectively.

6.2   Summary of main findings

The main findings from the follow-on study are:

- JOT is broadly supportive of the Welfare to Work Strategy. JOT itself supports and encourages the types of staff behaviour which are consistent with the Welfare to Work agenda, such as increasing the concentration on the hardest-to-help customers and generating more effective and sophisticated interventions to help this group of customers.

- The changes in behaviour and motivation of staff was widely welcomed in the organisation, though some Advisers and Adviser Managers still hanker after the simple certainties provided by the Daily Placing List and immediate, regular and outcome-based performance management information.

- However, it is difficult to isolate the impact of JOT due to the wide range of other changes in Jobcentre Plus. Many of these changes, such as the Channels Strategy were thought to be both consistent with JOT and consistent with the Welfare to Work Strategy. While supportive of them, JOT was not, though, thought to be **driving** the use of alternative service delivery channels.

- Some contextual changes, though, were thought to undermine or constrain the capacity of Jobcentre Plus to implement JOT effectively and for JOT to drive desired behaviours. In particular, instability and uncertainties in the levels and organisation of staffing have impacted in places on the capacity of JOT to drive individual and organisational change.

- The success of JOT is highly dependent on the capacity of key groups of staff to undertake appropriate and effective performance management. The evidence suggests that there are continued concerns about the capacity of Advisers and Adviser Managers to make the transition to using a broader range of quantitative and qualitative input information and to use individual coaching and support to help improve Adviser performance, though there has certainly been a renewed emphasis on these approaches as a result of JOT.

- There was some evidence that JOT is leading to more 'appropriate' submissions and referrals activity among Advisers.

- However, the introduction of the AAT and in particular the rather rigid submissions target within it was widely felt to be undermining the change in submissions activity and leading to a reliance among both Adviser Managers and more senior managers in the district and regional hierarchy of the organisation on narrow quantitative performance information to the detriment of the consistency of JOT with assisting the hardest-to-help customers find sustainable work. Underlining this, relatively little mention was made by respondents of the role or use of Key Management Indicators; again, suggesting an over-reliance on a narrow range of performance data.

- The AAT was also thought to be encouraging a JET-like approach of generating a high volume of submissions in the hope that some of these would result in a job outcome. There was also widespread dissatisfaction and frustration with this, and a widely reported feeling that such a change would be regressive and to some extent, in conflict with the objective of helping the hardest-to-help customers move into sustainable work.

- Customers themselves were largely unaware of JOT and do not appear to have noticed any consistent patterns of change in the level or quality of service offered by Jobcentre Plus which can be attributed to JOT. Where they have identified changes this is in relation to the use of self-service channels and the quality of vacancies on offer.

- The evidence suggests that there has been no perceptible impact of JOT on employers or providers. However, there is some concern over the service quality impacts of less frequent contact with employers.

6.3 Implications

These key findings suggest a number of implications for the development of policy and management procedures:

- The need for organisational and institutional stability in relation to staffing and organisational structures and in messages about appropriate staff behaviour. It is important to bear in mind that Jobcentre Plus has a deeply embedded organisational and cultural commitment to the use of performance indicators and within the organisation there is a tendency to utilise headline measures, despite some concerns about their quality. As such, additional care needs to be given to ensuring that performance management tools, like the AAT, are used appropriately and are accompanied by guidance which makes clear that a balanced approach to measuring individual and team performance is most effective and that under JOT, qualitative performance management is at least as important as the use of quantitative headline data.

- To continue to clarify and reinforce messages with staff about the linkages between JOT and the wider organisational objectives of Jobcentre Plus in relation to the government's Welfare to Work Strategy and the initiatives within Jobcentre Plus that support this such as the Channels Strategy and approaches to employer engagement. These messages need to clearly establish the assumptions about what inputs lead to desirable outcomes and managers throughout the hierarchy of the organisation are to ensure that frontline delivery reflects these.

- Review AAT and its relationship with JOT in particular ensuring that managers through all layers of the hierarchy understand and accept the need for a broader and balanced approach to the use of both quantitative and qualitative information.

- Continued improvement of self-help channels to ensure that these are able to cope with increased demand and satisfy the needs of customers, avoiding 'bounce-back' to face-to-face channels and disillusionment with job search.

- Continued emphasis on building and sustaining staff and organisational capacity in support of the emphasis of JOT on desirable behaviour. At Adviser level this relates to the types of advice, submissions and referrals behaviour desired and the skills and knowledge required to implement this. At Adviser Manager level this relates to the capacity of Adviser Managers to undertake qualitative assessment, interpret a range of quantitative input data and to support, coach and mentor individual and groups of Advisers. At district and regional level, this involves an understanding of the messages and meaning of performance data and the need to consider this in relation to other more qualitative information and the need to give appropriate guidance and support to staff lower down in the hierarchy in using this.

- Attention will need to be given to the skills of the new Adviser Managers and to ensuring that they have the skills and experience necessary to operate effectively in a JOT environment.

- Continual review of the impact of JOT on employer contact/customer service. In particular, staff need to be supported in maintaining appropriate levels of contact with employers to ensure that the two-way flow of information is sufficient for employers' needs to be met and Jobcentre Plus staff to understand the local labour market and to be able to target small scale follow-up activities to support customers and identify customers who may not be fulfilling their obligations to seek work.

Appendix A
Changes to Jobcentre Plus workforce

Figure A.1   New Jobcentre Plus customer service workforce structure

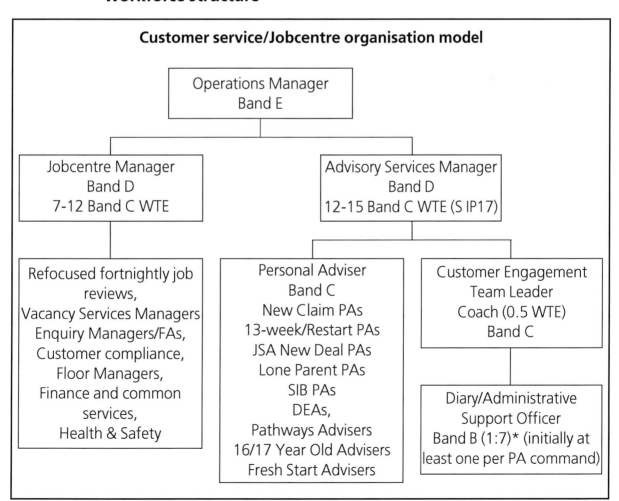

Figure A.2   Letter to Jobcentre Plus staff, explaining changes to the staffing structure

25 May 2006

To: everyone in Jobcentre Plus

Re: New Customer Service/Jobcentre Organisation Model

I wanted to let you know about the new Customer Service/Jobcentre Standard Organisation Model. The model sees the introduction of new Band D Advisory Services Manager and Jobcentre Manager roles in 95% of Jobcentres across Jobcentre Plus.

The Advisory Services Manager will be accountable for improving the quality, productivity and performance of welfare to work advisory services. The Jobcentre Manager will be accountable for the effective delivery of individual and employer customer service, JSA conditionality and Customer Compliance.

The job role profiles are explained in detail in the following link (Job Role Profiles). Please take time to look at them and to think about how they will support the work you do. The new functional split of line management responsibilities recognises the breadth and complexity of Jobcentre business. It will also provide a consistent organisational platform for introducing standard processes across our customer services business. Overall, this will mean 250 additional Band D Manager jobs in Jobcentres and promotion opportunities where these vacancies cannot be filled by substantive DWP staff. Directors will be writing to you in the coming weeks to give details around vacancy/post filling arrangements locally. I am convinced that these changes will help us focus even more successfully on the targets we have been set for 2006/07. The opportunities presented by these new roles will be good news for the majority of you but I do understand that Band C Advisor Managers and Senior Advisers will be disappointed and will want to know what this means for them. I have asked my Regional/Country Directors to write to individual Band C and D Managers who are directly impacted by the new roles, explaining the changes and next steps, and to follow this up with face to face meetings between each person affected and their line manager over the coming week. You have clearly told us that you want your Senior Managers to tell you personally about changes that impact on you and we are doing that. I am also attaching answers to some general questions about the new model covering:

Why are we doing this? What are the roles? What are the timescales? How can I apply? What will happen to me?

I hope that these arrangements will give you the information you need about the new Jobcentre Organisational Model. Where you feel this is not the case, please let me know preferably by email. Over the coming months I hope to chat to a number of you about the impact of these changes on our customer delivery.

Figure A.3   Questions about the new staffing structure

Why are we doing this?

The introduction of the new standard organisational model is a vital step in helping to transform our services to customers. It will provide a common platform for standard processes developed under the SOM and enable us to deliver more consistent customer focused services across all of our Jobcentres.

What benefits will this bring?

Key Benefits:

- Providing stronger managerial and administrative support to enable us to achieve our stretching performance targets and improve the productivity of our advisory services.

- Enables Jobcentre Managers to focus on improving JSA conditionality, compliance & individual and employer customer service.

- Focusing Personal Advisers purely on advisory work and moving any non-advisory work to other roles.

- Introducing Diary/Administrative Support Officers to be the first point of contact for customers phoning into the Advisory Team.

- Providing technical and procedural support to the Advisory Services Manager through a new Band C Customer Engagement Team Leader post, helping in the delivery of the new KMIs.

- Supporting deployment of the new Quality Assurance Framework.

- Improved Learning & Development route ways.

What are the new roles?

The standard model introduces 4 new job roles:

- Jobcentre Manager - Band D

- Adviser Manager - Band D

- Customer Engagement Team Leader- Band C

- Diary/Administrative Support Band B Officer

What are the timescales?

The new organisational model should be rolled out by the end of September 2006. This is a key enabler to further improvements in the JSA regime and welfare to work Advisory Services, so we want to move quickly to the new design. By introducing the model this year, we will begin to realise the benefits of improved customer service and productivity within this operational year. Directors and HR have been consulted on timeframes.

Will the model apply to all Jobcentres?

Nationally the model will be applied in full in at least 95% of all Jobcentres. Your line manager will be able to give you more detail of how the model will look in your district/region/country.

How much will this cost?

The new Jobcentre Standard Organisational model is a significant investment in managerial and administrative support. There will be an initial cost in the 1st year (just under £2 million), but this will be outweighed by improvements in performance and productivity as the new model takes effect.

Does this mean there will be more Band D posts in Jobcentres?

Yes. Nationally there will be about 250 additional Band D posts in Jobcentres and promotion opportunities where these vacancies cannot be filled by substantive DWP staff. How can I apply for one of the new roles? Normal DWP vacancy/post filling arrangements will apply. Your Director will be writing out to you soon to explain the vacancy/post filling arrangements for your local area. Directors have written to individual Band C and D managers who are directly impacted by the new roles, explaining the changes and next steps. This will be followed by face-to-face meetings with line managers over the coming week or so.

Has the model been tested?

Yes. The basic functional approach to organisation has been introduced in East of England, Yorkshire and the Humber and Scotland and their experiences have been used to inform the model.

How will the success of the change be evaluated?

Each district will nominate a lead command that will provide feedback on the implementation process and business benefits. Has TU been consulted? Yes. National TU have been consulted and have commented on the new job role profiles and implementation plans.

Appendix B
Topic guide for Jobcentre Plus staff

Discussion guide: Jobcentre Plus managers and staff

Note to interviewers: The guide covers a wide range of topics and it is not expected that every topic will be covered in depth in every interview. Judgement should be used in ensuring that the most appropriate questions are asked of each respondent/group and that interviews should last **no more than one hour**.

Questions most relevant to managers are marked **M**. Questions that should be asked of staff respondents are marked **S**.

NB: where reference is made to priority groups, please take specific note of which priority group is being discussed.

1 Background, target setting, communication and understanding of JOT

1.1	M	What **issues specific to this district** (local labour market, organisational or otherwise) do you believe to have had an impact on JOT performance and delivery? In what ways?
1.2	M	To what extent and in what ways have **national issues** such as ODR and changes in resource level affected performance and delivery under JOT?
1.3	M	Please describe the way in which the **JOT targets** for 2006-07 were established?

1.4	M	In what ways have **changes in target levels** for 2006-07 affected planning and management behaviour compared with the Pilot period?
1.5	MS	Describe how these were **communicated** to staff and how any issues arising were addressed.
1.6	MS	In the light of the above, how well do staff now **understand** the Pilot target system, as compared with January 2005 when the JOT Pilot started?
1.7	MS	In what ways has the **national roll-out** helped to improve staff understanding of JOT?

2   Changes in working practices

Ask as open question and probe/prompt as appropriate to role of respondent

Focus as closely as possible on the specific impact on working practices of <u>JOT</u>

Open questions		
2.1	MS	What changes have occurred in working practices since the introduction of JOT in this district in January 2005?
2.2	MS	What additional changes have occurred since the national roll-out of JOT in April 2006?
<div align="center">**Prompts** (*as appropriate to respondent*)</div>		
Follow up with employers and customers		
2.3	MS	To what extent are staff **'chasing destinations'** despite the fact that this is no longer necessary? If they are, why is this?
2.4	MS	Have there been any changes in the **process** for dealing with people who advise Jobcentre Plus that they have got a job (*e.g. spec subs, 'end of week' rush, ADF*)?
2.5	M	Are staff still following up submissions with employers? If so why?
2.6	MS	In particular (how) has the use of the Adviser Discretion Fund (**ADF**) been affected by JOT?
2.7	MS	Have there been any changes in the way that **teams** within the district are working together?

| 2.8 | M | In particular, has there been any change in the working relationship between **job-broking and benefit-processing staff**? |
| 2.9 | MS | Has there been any change in the working relationship between **advisers and frontline staff**? (e.g. re referral of customers)? |

Customer service

2.10	MS	What changes have there been in relation to the treatment of **non-claimants** and/or **job-ready customers**? (e.g. increased direction to self-help channels)? How are these groups identified? What role is played by floorwalkers, frontline staff etc? Any changes in help provided to customers re using self-help channels? **(Focus on JSA Action Plan**)
2.11	MS	What changes have there been in the way in which **'harder to help'** groups are being treated? In particular, has there been an increase in 'work focus' as a result of JOT? How does this manifest itself (changes in procedures, link with JSA interventions etc.)?
2.12	MS	Specifically, are staff **spending more time** with harder to help customers
2.13	MS	Do staff feel that there is an increase in the **quality of service** to harder to help customers (and what evidence can they cite to support this)?
2.14	M	Overall, what has been the impact of JOT on **customer service** for the different groups? Any evidence to back up statements?

Submissions

2.15	M	Has there been any noticeable change in the practice of **submissions** for vacancies (e.g. fewer spec/ordinary submissions; more targeted submissions than existed under JET)?
2.16	MS	Any change in the **type of jobs** for which customers have been submitted (e.g. part time, low paid,)?
2.17	M	Any feedback from **employers** re quantity and/or quality of submissions?

Referrals to providers

| 2.18 | M | Has the frequency of referrals to providers changed? If so why/how? |
| 2.19 | M | Has the type of customers being referred changed? If so, why/how? |

2.20	M	Is there any evidence of staff referring clients to a broader range of **provision** than that currently formally contracted? Is there any evidence of change in the way in which the district is **working with providers**?
2.21	M	Has there been any change in the relation with **employment agencies** as a result of JOT?
Relations with employers		
2.22	MS	How has JOT affected the way in which the district works with **employers**?
2.23	MS	Has there been any changes in relation to **recruitment events**, job fairs etc?
2.24	M	Has there been any feedback from employers about **reduced follow-up**? Is this positive/negative/neutral?
Overall		
2.25	S	Do staff believe that they are now **working more effectively** under JOT?
2.26	S	What **unexpected consequences** have arisen as a result of JOT?

3   Motivation, behaviour and skills

Note: questions should relate to the Adviser Achievement Tool and other changes in JSA interventions since April 2006. Try to pick up differences in perspectives between managers and staff.		
3.1	MS	In what ways has the move away from **individual targets** affected staff motivation? Does this vary between staff groups?
3.2	MS	Do **advisers** use their **time** differently as a result of changes to the target system? If so, how?
3.3	MS	Do staff feel that the introduction of JOT provides sufficient incentives for them to prioritise harder to help customers?
3.4	M	Is there any evidence so far of more effective **team working** as a result of JOT?
3.5	MS	Are there any noticeable differences in the way that staff **relate to customers? Employers? Providers? Partners?**
3.6	M	Has JOT had any other noticeable impact so far on **staff motivation or behaviour**?

3.7	MS	Specifically, are staff more willing to refer job-ready customers to self help channels? If not, why?
3.8	MS	Are staff more willing to refer job-ready customers to Jobcentre Plus Direct now? If not why?
3.9	MS	In particular, are there still queues at warm phones or do customers directed to self-help channels still return to the Jobcentre Plus office for face-to-face help? If so why?
3.10	S	How are staff **monitoring** their own performance?
3.11	MS	How do staff perceive that their individual performance **contributes** to the overall achievement of the JOT target?
3.12	M	To what extent and in what ways do **efficiency and productivity** issues impinge on the ability of individuals and teams to contribute towards the achievement of the JOT target?

4   Overall opinions of JOT

4.1	M	To what extent and in what ways has JOT affected the delivery of **other Jobcentre Plus targets** (CST, OST, MVFE, BDT)
4.2	MS	Overall, what are the **benefits** of the JOT system?
4.3	MS	Overall, what are the **drawbacks** of the system?
4.4	MS	Are there any **improvements** that could be suggested to the operation of JOT?
4.5	MS	Are there any **other issues** that you would like to raise regarding JOT that we have not covered during this discussion?

Appendix C
Topic guide for employers

Discussion guide: employers

Evaluation of Job Outcome Target (JOT) Pilots

One year follow up study

Topic guide for interviews with employers

Note to interviewers: *In order to minimise the burden on employers, it is important that the interview is kept to a maximum of* **20 minutes** *unless it is clear that the respondent is happy to talk for longer than this.*

As a filter, all employers should be asked if they have used Jobcentre Plus services in the last twelve months prior to arranging an interview.

---

1   Use of Jobcentre Plus services

1.1   Which Jobcentre Plus services have you used **in the last 12 months** (i.e. since July 2005)? (PROMPT IF NECESSARY)

   1.1.1   Placed vacancies in Jobcentre Plus office-how many?

   1.1.2   Placed vacancies through Apply Direct- how many?

   1.1.3   Attended job fair or other recruitment event

   1.1.4   Conducted large-scale recruitment exercise

   1.1.5   Used Jobcentre Plus office to conduct interviews

   1.1.6   Other

1.2   Which of these services did you use **during 2004** or earlier? (PROMPT AS ABOVE)

1.3 Did you notice any **difference in the service that you received** between 2004 and the most recent time that you used the service(s)? (PROMPT IF NECESSARY)

    1.3.1   Contact with Jobcentre Plus sales staff

    1.3.2   Contact with Jobcentre Plus local office staff

    1.3.3   Contact with Jobcentre Plus call centres

    1.3.4   Quality of labour market knowledge of Jobcentre Plus staff (and does this match their needs)?

    1.3.5   Quantity and quality of job applicants submitted by Jobcentre Plus ***(PROBE FULLY)***

    1.3.6   Time taken to fill vacancy

    1.3.7   Level of bureaucracy involved

    1.3.8   Telephone follow-up ***(PROBE FULLY)***

1.4 Have any of these changes affected your working relationship with Jobcentre Plus? If so, how and why?

1.5 In general, would you say that the quality of the service that you have received from Jobcentre Plus has improved, declined or remained about the same recently? What are the reasons for your response?

2   Awareness/understanding of Jobcentre Plus target system

2.1 Are you aware that Jobcentre Plus operates a target system?

2.2 If, so please outline briefly your understanding of how this system works

2.3 Are you aware that (NAME OF DISTRICT) district has been piloting a new target system since January 2005?

2.4 Are you aware that a new target system (JOT) was implemented by Jobcentre Plus nationally in April 2006? If so, when and how did you become aware?

2.5 If, so please outline briefly your understanding of how this system works

2.6 (If aware of JOT) do you feel that the new system has impacted on your relationship with Jobcentre Plus? If so, how?

3   Other comments about recent service received from Jobcentre Plus

4 Basic details

4.1 Name of respondent

4.2 Position of respondent

4.3 Sector

4.4 Size of establishment (no. of employees) at the site and across the whole organisation. Note here whether interaction with Jobcentre Plus is managed at this site or by another office within the organisation?

4.5 Independent or part of group?

Appendix D
Topic guide for interviews with providers

Evaluation of Job Outcome Target (JOT) Pilots

Stage 4: Option one follow-up

Topic guide for interviews with providers (both contracted and non-contracted)

> **Note to interviewers**: *In order to minimise the burden on respondents, it is important that the interview is kept to a <u>maximum</u> of 30 minutes unless it is clear that the respondent is happy to talk for longer than this.*

4 Contact with Jobcentre Plus
4.1 What dealings have you had with Jobcentre Plus **since April 2006** (PROMPT IF NECESSARY)

    4.1.1 Discussion/negotiation of contracts

    4.1.2 Referral of Jobcentre Plus customers to programmes

    4.1.3 Contact re quality assurance (DPQMT)

    4.1.4 Contact re monitoring of customer progress

    4.1.5 Placement of customers into jobs

    4.1.6 Other

4.2   Have you noticed any **changes in the nature of your contact with Jobcentre Plus** since April 2006? (PROMPT IF NECESSARY)

    4.2.1   Contact with Jobcentre Plus local office staff

    4.2.2   Contact with Jobcentre Plus advisers

    *4.2.3   (**Contracted providers only**) Contact with DPQMT*

    *4.2.4   (**Contracted providers only**) Quantity and methods of customer tracking (including who is responsible for this). [**NOTE**: this is a key topic – please probe as necessary e.g. are the new systems affecting the measured performance of the provider?]*

    4.2.5   Quantity and quality of referrals

    4.2.6   Level of bureaucracy involved e.g. form-filling, telephone follow-up etc.

        Probe: Is this reduced, are they asked for less information by Jobcentre Plus

    4.2.7   Frequency of contact with Jobcentre Plus

    4.2.8   Interest of Jobcentre Plus staff in the type and range of provision available and relative success rates

5   Awareness/understanding of Jobcentre Plus Target system

5.1   Are you aware that Jobcentre Plus operates a target system?

5.2   If, so please outline briefly your understanding of how this system works

5.3   Are you aware that Jobcentre Plus introduced a new target system (Job Outcome Target – JOT) in April 2006?
[**NOTE**: *all contracted providers should have received a letter from Clive Mitchell, Acting Director of Provision and Partnerships*]

5.4   If, so please outline briefly your understanding of how this system works

5.5   (If aware of JOT) do you feel that the new system has impacted on your relationship with Jobcentre Plus? If so, how?

6   Other comments about recent contact with Jobcentre Plus

Probe for performance issues and whether they think they are judged fairly by Jobcentre Plus.

Do they think they are still seen as being important for Jobcentre Plus delivery.

7   Basic details

7.1   Name of respondent

7.2   Position of respondent

7.3   Service provided

7.4   Type of organisation e.g. private, voluntary, community, college etc.

7.5   Independent or part of group?

7.6   Contracted or non-contracted?

Appendix E
Topic guide for PG1/2/3
Customer Focus Groups

Job Outcome Target Option 1 Pilots one year on

Customer Focus Group topic guide

1)   Introductions

Introduce team members

Outline research aims

Ask participants to introduce themselves

2)   Interaction with Jobcentre Plus

How often do you usually contact Jobcentre Plus

How do you usually contact Jobcentre Plus

Why do you usually contact Jobcentre Plus

How long have you been attending your usual Jobcentre Plus site

Are you currently looking for work

3)   Change in Service

Over the past 12 months (*or if less than 12 months*, during the time you have been attending your usual site) have you noticed any difference in the service provided by Jobcentre Plus

4) Change in Service (Staff Contact)

Specifically in the last 12 months (*or if less than 12 months*, during the time you have been attending your usual site) have you noticed a difference in:

i) The amount of contact with you have with **frontline Jobcentre Plus** staff (eg the floorwalkers, receptionists and (for PG2 & 3 only) fortnightly review staff

Do you spend more/less time with frontline staff than you did previously

Are they more or less available to help you than they were before

ii) The amount of contact with you have with **Jobcentre Plus Advisers** (eg Lone Parent Advisers, New Deal Advisers and Personal Advisers)

Do you meet your adviser more or less often than before

Do you spend more/less time with Advisers than you did previously

Do you feel that your meetings with your adviser are more or less work focused than before ie:

For PG2 & 3s ask:

- Do you spend more or less time discussing job options **(PG2 & 3)**

- Do you apply for more or less vacancies than before **(PG2 & 3)**

- Are you contacted at home about vacancies more or less often than before **(PG2 & 3)**

- Do you discuss being referred to other agencies (eg for training to help you return to work) more or less often than before **(PG2 & 3)**

- Have you been referred to other agencies (eg for training) more or less often than before **(PG2 & 3)**

For PG1s ask:

- Do you spend more or less time discussing the possibility of returning to work **(PG1)**

- Do you spend more or less time discussing the job options available to you **(PG1)**

- Do you discuss being referred to other agencies (eg for training to help you return to work) more or less often than before **(PG1)**

- Have you been referred to other agencies (eg for training) more or less often than before **(PG1)**

Ask All

Do you spend more or less time discussing non work focused issues (eg queries about benefits etc) with your adviser than did were before

In general do you feel you get enough support about non work focused issues

iii)   Have you noticed any change in your contact with any other Jobcentre Plus staff

5)   Change in Service (Systems)

Only ask the PG1s the questions if any of them are looking for work

In the last 12 months (**or if less than 12 months**, during the time you have been attending your usual site) have you noticed any difference in your use of 'self service' channels in the Jobcentre (eg Warm phones in offices, **Jobpoints,** Jobcentre Plus Website etc)

Do you use them more/less often than before

Why are you using the warm phones more/less often than before

Why are you using the Jobpoints more/less often than before

Why are you using the Jobcentre Plus website more/less often than before

Are you happy/confident to use them

Do you feel you get enough support/instruction in how to use them

Would you prefer to deal with a staff member face to face than use these channels

If yes: Why do you prefer to deal with a staff member face to face than use these channels

If no: Why do you prefer to use these channels than deal with a staff member face to face

Have you noticed any other changes related to using the self service channels

6)   Change in Service (Vacancies)

Only ask the PG1s this section if any of them are looking for work

Again in the last 12 months (**or if less than 12 months**, during the time you have been attending your usual site) have you noticed any difference in:

The types/quantity/quality of vacancies available in the Jobcentre

The types/quantity/quality of vacancies you are submitted for by the Jobcentre

The amount of time Jobcentre Plus staff spend with you discussing vacancies

The way you apply for vacancies ie do you use employer direct or do staff do this for you

Have you noticed any other changes related to vacancies

7) Awareness of JOT

Did you know that Jobcentre Plus operates a target system for getting people back into work

Did you know that in January 2005 this district was chosen to test a new type of target system for getting people back into work

If yes, how did you find out about the new system

If yes, do you know how the new system works

Did you know that in April 2006 this new target system for getting people back into work was rolled out to include all Jobcentre Plus sites

If yes, how did you find out about this

8) Satisfaction with the Service

Over the last 12 months (*or if less than 12 months*, during the time you have been attending your usual site) do you think the service you have received from Jobcentre Plus had got better or worse

Why

Overall how satisfied are you with the service you currently receive compared to that you received 12 months ago (*or if less than 12 months*, during the time you have been attending your usual site)?

Why

9) Any other comments about the Service

Appendix F
Questionnaire for traffic survey of PG4/5 customers

DISTRICT ID		
ID NUMBER		

 leeds metropolitan university

Job Outcome Targets Face to Face
Customer Survey Questionnaire 2006

Introduction

Hello, my name is XXXX, and I am from Leeds Metropolitan University. We are currently conducting a survey on behalf of Jobcentre Plus to find out what people are using this office for today and to see if they have noticed any changes to the service provided by Jobcentre Plus in the last year or so.

Would you be willing to take part in an interview? It will only take around 5 to 10 minutes to complete.

Say as necessary - all replies are completely confidential and cannot be linked to individuals. Results are given to Jobcentre Plus as statistics only and the study cannot affect any benefits you may be claiming.

Interviewer Name:
....

Jobcentre Plus Office:
....

Date of Interview:
....

Duration of Interview:
....

Jobcentre Plus District	ID
Calderdale and Kirklees	01
Devon	02
Lambeth, Southwark and Wandsworth	03
North West Wales and Powys	04

Screening Questions

1   Just before we start the survey can I ask: Are you currently in work? **CODE ONE ONLY**

      1   YES   *(Go to Question 3)*   2   NO

2   How long have you been out of work? (in months) **PROMPT FOR AN APPROXIMATION**

3   Are you currently claiming any benefits?   **CODE ONE OPTION ONLY**

      1   YES   *(Go to Question 4)*   2   NO

4   Which benefits are you claiming? **CODE ALL THAT APPLY**

    1   Jobseekers Allowance (JSA)
    2   Income Support (IS)
    3   Incapacity Benefit (IB)
    4   Severe Disablement Allowance
    5   Maternity Allowance
    6   Bereavement Benefits
    7   Industrial Injuries Disablement Benefit
    8   Carer's Allowance
    9   Tax Credits
   10   Training Allowance
   11   Disability Living Allowance (DLA)
   12   Housing Benefit
   13   Council Tax Benefit
   14   Other *(Please Specify)*...
   15   None
   16   Don't know / Can't remember
   17   Prefer Not To Say

If the respondent is IN WORK and NOT CLAIMING JSA, IB or IS continue (PG5)

If the respondent is IN WORK and is CLAIMING JSA, IB or IS terminate the interview

If the respondent is NOT IN WORK and NOT CLAIMING JSA, IB or IS continue (PG4)

If the respondent is NOT IN WORK and is CLAIMING JSA, IB or IS terminate the interview

Section A: Your use of the Jobcentre Plus Office

5. Could you tell me the main reason why you visited this Jobcentre Plus office today?

DO NOT PROMPT, CODE ONE ONLY

1	TO LOOK FOR JOB VACANCIES
2	TO ASK ABOUT JOB VACANCIES
3	TO ATTEND AN INTERVIEW WITH AN ADVISER
4	TO REGISTER AS UNEMPLOYED / MAKE NEW CLAIM FOR BENEFIT
5	TO ENQUIRE HOW TO QUALIFY FOR/ CLAIM FOR UNEMPLOYMENT AND/ OR OTHER BENEFITS (SUCH AS INCAPACITY BENEFIT, DISABILITY BENEFIT ETC)
6	TO ASK ABOUT EMPLOYMENT OR TRAINING SCHEMES
7	TO ASK ABOUT A JOB RELATED MATTER (NOT A VACANCY ENQUIRY)
8	TO MAKE AN APPOINTMENT / ARRANGE AN INTERVIEW WITH STAFF
9	TO MAKE A COMPLAINT
10	OTHER **(PLEASE SPECIFY)** ....

6. And did you do anything else whilst here today?

DO NOT PROMPT AND CODE ALL THAT APPLY

1	I LOOKED FOR JOB VACANCIES
2	I ASKED ABOUT JOB VACANCIES
3	I ATTENDED AN INTERVIEW WITH AN ADVISER
4	I REGISTERED AS UNEMPLOYED / MADE NEW CLAIM FOR BENEFIT
5	I ENQUIRED HOW TO QUALIFY FOR/ CLAIM FOR UNEMPLOYMENT AND/ OR OTHER BENEFITS (SUCH AS INCAPACITY BENEFIT, DISABILITY BENEFIT ETC)
6	I ASKED ABOUT EMPLOYMENT OR TRAINING SCHEMES
7	I ASKED ABOUT A JOB RELATED MATTER (NOT A VACANCY ENQUIRY)
8	I MADE AN APPOINTMENT / ARRANGE AN INTERVIEW WITH STAFF
9	I MADE A COMPLAINT
10	OTHER **(PLEASE SPECIFY)** ....
11	**NOTHING ELSE**

7. If you have not established in Questions 5 and 6 whether the person is looking for a job or not ask: Are you currently looking for work / a new job?

CODE ONE OPTION ONLY

1   YES

2   NO *(Go to Question 20)*

8. How often do you visit this, or other local Jobcentre Plus offices in the area, to look for vacancies?
   PROMPT FOR AN APPROXIMATION AND CODE ONE ONLY

   1 DAILY
   2 MORE THAN ONCE A WEEK
   3 ONCE A WEEK
   4 ONCE A FORTNIGHT
   5 ONCE A MONTH
   6 THREE OR FOUR TIMES A YEAR
   7 TWICE A YEAR
   8 ONCE A YEAR
   9 OCCASIONALLY *(LESS THAN ONCE A YEAR)*
   10 JUST STARTED VISITING *(FIRST OR SECOND VISIT)*

Section B: Use of Jobcentre Plus Jobsearch Services

9. A) Which of the following have you used when looking for vacancies in the Jobcentre, have you......? **CODE EITHER YES OR NO FOR EACH IN COLUMN A**

   B) If more than one used ask: And which of these do you use most often when looking for vacancies in the jobcentre, is it......? **READ OUT THOSE USED AND CODE WHICH _ONE_ IS USED MOST OFTEN IN COLUMN B**

   C) If more than one used ask: And which of these do you prefer to use when looking for vacancies in the jobcentre, is it......? **READ OUT THOSE USED AND CODE WHICH _ONE_ IS PREFERRED IN COLUMN C**

	a		b	c
JOBSEARCH METHOD	YES	NO	OFTEN	PREFER
1. Used the Jobpoints	1	2	1	1
2. looked at the jobcentre plus internet site	1	2	2	2
3. Looked at THE jobcentre plus vacancy lists / books / newspapers	1	2	3	3
4. Searched for vacancies with a jobcentre plus adviser	1	2	4	4
5. Phones Jobseeker direct and asked them to do the initial search for vacancies for you	1	2	5	5
6. Other (Please specify)	1	2	6	6
7. More than one/can't decide			7	7
8. Don't know			8	8

10.   If preference was given in Q9C ask: Why do you prefer to look for vacancies this way?

    Insert Preference Number From Previous Question (eg 1 for Jobpoints) :............

11.   When looking for vacancies in the Jobcentre, do you think you get enough help and support?

CODE ONE OPTION ONLY

1   YES   **(GO TO Q13)**
2   NO   **(GO TO Q12)**
3   DON'T KNOW / CAN'T REMEMBER **(GO TO Q13)**
4   NOT APPLICABLE (EG IF FIRST VISIT) **(GO TO Q13)**

12.   If no ask: What additional help and support would you like to receive?
PROMPT AND CODE ALL THAT APPLY

1	More opportunity to carry out face to face jobsearch with staff
2	more time to carry out face to face jobsearch with staff
3	more support / instruction when using the self help channels
4	more GUIDANCE FROM STAFF ABOUT HOW TO FOLLOW UP VACANCIES
5	Other (Please specify) ……… ……… ……… ………
6	Don't Know

13.   Have you ever found a vacancy in the Jobcentre that you've wanted to follow up (ie find out more about /apply for)?

CODE ONE OPTION ONLY

1   YES   **(GO TO Q14)**
2   NO   **(GO TO Q18)**
3   DON'T KNOW / CAN'T REMEMBER **(GO TO Q18)**
4   NOT APPLICABLE (EG IF FIRST VISIT) **(GO TO Q18)**

14.   A) Which of the following methods have you used when following up a jobcentre vacancy that you were interested in, have you……? **CODE EITHER YES OR NO FOR EACH IN COLUMN A**

B) If more than one used ask: And which of these methods do you use most often when following up a vacancy, is it……? **READ OUT THOSE USED AND CODE WHICH _ONE_ IS USED MOST OFTEN IN COLUMN B**

C) If more than one used ask: And which of these do you prefer to use when following up a vacancy, is it……?   **READ OUT THOSE USED AND CODE WHICH _ONE_ IS PREFERRED IN COLUMN C**

JOBSEARCH METHOD	a		b	c
	YES	NO	OFTEN	PREFER
1. discussed a vacancy face to face with an adviser in the office	1	2	1	1
2. rung jobseeker direct using the jobcentre plus phones	1	2	2	2
3. rung jobseeker direct but not used the jobcentre plus phones eg from home	1	2	3	3
4. rung an employer direct using the jobcentre plus phones	1	2	4	4
5. rung an employer direct but not used the jobcentre plus phones eg from home	1	2	5	5
6. looked for more information on the vacancy using the jobcentre plus website	1	2	6	6
7. Other (Please specify)	1	2	7	7
8. More than one/can't decide			8	8
9. Don't know			9	9

15. If preference was given in Q14C ask: Why do you prefer to follow up vacancies this way?

   Insert Preference Number From Previous Question (eg 1 for Jobpoints) :............
   ....

16. When following up vacancies, do you think you get enough help and support from Jobcentre Plus?

   CODE ONE OPTION ONLY

   1   YES   **(GO TO Q18)**
   2   NO   **(GO TO Q17)**
   3   DON'T KNOW / CAN'T REMEMBER **(GO TO Q18)**
   4   NOT APPLICABLE (EG IF FIRST VISIT) **(GO TO Q18)**

17. If no ask: What additional help and support would you like to receive?
   PROMPT AND CODE ALL THAT APPLY

1	MORE OPPORTUNITY TO TALK FACE TO FACE WITH THE STAFF ABOUT VACANCIES YOU ARE INTERESTED IN
2	MORE TIME TO TALK TO THE STAFF ABOUT VACANCIES YOU ARE INTERESTED IN
3	MORE INFORMATION ON HOW TO FOLLOW UP A VACANCY
4	OTHER (PLEASE SPECIFY) ....
5	DON'T KNOW

18. Overall, how satisfied are you with the Jobsearch services provided by Jobcentre Plus?

    CODE ONE OPTION ONLY

    1 VERY SATISFIED **(GO TO Q20)**
    2 SATISFIED **(GO TO Q20)**
    3 NEITHER SATISFIED NOR DISSATISFIED **(GO TO Q20)**
    4 DISSATISFIED **(GO TO Q19)**
    5 VERY DISSATISFIED **(GO TO Q19)**
    6 DON'T KNOW / CAN'T REMEMBER **(GO TO Q20)**

19. Why are you dissatisfied with the Jobsearch services provided by Jobcentre Plus?

    ....

Section C: Changes in Service

20. How long have you been visiting this or other local Jobcentre Plus offices in the area?

    CODE ONE OPTION ONLY

    1 LESS THAN 1 MONTH **(Go to Q26)**
    2 BETWEEN 1 AND 3 MONTHS **(Go to Q26)**
    3 BETWEEN 3 AND 6 MONTHS **(Go to Q21)**
    4 BETWEEN 6 AND 12 MONTHS **(Go to Q21)**
    5 BETWEEN 1 AND 2 YEARS **(Go to Q21)**
    6 BETWEEN 2 AND 5 YEARS **(Go to Q21)**
    7 MORE THAN 5 YEARS **(Go to Q21)**
    8 DON'T KNOW / CAN'T REMEMBER **(Go to Q21)**

21. Have you noticed any differences or changes in the service provided by Jobcentre Plus between this time last year (or your earliest contact with Jobcentre Plus if sooner) and the last 3 or 4 months (ie since April this year).

    (Interviewers MUST ensure that the respondent has understood the timescales before asking the following questions.)

    CODE ONE OPTION ONLY

    1 YES **(GO TO Q22)**
    2 NO **(GO TO Q23)**
    3 DON'T KNOW / CAN'T REMEMBER **(GO TO Q23)**

22. What differences have you noticed?

    DO NOT PROMPT & CODE ALL THAT APPLY

1	There are more staff available to help you than before
2	There are Less staff available to help you than before
3	It's harder to get to talk to staff about vacancies
4	It's easier to get to talk to staff about vacancies
5	You are encouraged to use the self service channels more
6	You are encouraged to use the self service channels Less
7	Other (Please specify) ....
8	Don't Know

23. Between this time last year (or your earliest contact with Jobcentre Plus if sooner) and the last 3 or 4 months (ie since April this year) do you think that the service you received from Jobcentre Plus got better, worse or stayed the same?

    CODE ONE OPTION ONLY

    1   BETTER **(GO TO Q24)**
    2   WORSE   **(GO TO Q25)**
    3   STAYED THE SAME **(GO TO Q26)**
    4   DON'T KNOW / CAN'T REMEMBER **(GO TO Q26)**

24. In what ways is it better?

    PROBE FOR DIFFERENCES

    ....
    ....*Go to Q26*

25. In what ways is it worse?

    PROBE FOR DIFFERENCES

    ....

26. Finally do you have any other comments you'd like to make about the service you receive from Jobcentre Plus?

    ....

Section D: Respondent Details

27. I'd now like to ask you a few details about yourself for classification purposes only.

Record Gender   **DO NOT ASK:**

    1   MALE   2   FEMALE

28. Do you have any long term illness, health problem or disability which limits your daily activities or the work you can do?

    CODE ONE OPTION ONLY

    1   YES   2   NO   3   PREFER NOT TO SAY

29. Are you a single / lone parent (with children up to 16 years of age)?

    CODE ONE OPTION ONLY

    1   YES   2   NO   3   PREFER NOT TO SAY

30. Which of the following best describes your ethnic background?

CODE ONE OPTION ONLY

White		Black	
White – British	☐ 1	Caribbean	☐ 12
White – Irish	☐ 2	African	☐ 13
Other White background (Please specify)	☐ 3	Other Black background (Please specify)	☐ 14
Mixed		**Chinese or other ethnic group**	
White and Black Caribbean	☐ 4	Chinese	☐ 15
White and Black African	☐ 5		
White and Asian	☐ 6		
Other Mixed background (Please specify)	☐ 7	Other (Please specify)	☐ 16
Asian or Asian British		**No response**	
Indian	☐ 8	I do not wish to say	☐ 17
Pakistani	☐ 9		
Bangladeshi	☐ 10	Don't know	☐ 18
Any other Asian background (Please specify)	☐ 11		

THANK RESPONDENT AND CLOSE